NOBODY EATS PARSLEY

NOBODY EATS PARSLEY

And other things I learned from my family

David Oakley

CARMEL
SAYBROOK
BOOKS

This book is an original production of Carmel Saybrook Publishing

Carmel Saybrook Publishing
1445 S. Mint Street
Charlotte, NC 28203

Cover design by Laura Beebe
Cover photograph by Mike Carroll
Interior design by Diana Wade

I have tried to recreate events, locales, and conversations from
my memories of them. In order to maintain anonymity in some
instances, I have changed the names of individuals and places, and
I may have changed some identifying characteristics and details,
such as physical properties, occupations, and places of residence.

ISBN 978-0-578-75726-1

For Claire, Sydney, Lucas, and the rest of my family for giving me so much fun stuff to write about.

CONTENTS

INTRODUCTION

I've been a collector my whole life.

Autographs, stamps, baseball cards, poker chips, hotel room keys, lunch boxes, matchbooks, bottle caps, paint-by-number paintings, and credit cards. Yes, I have a vintage credit card collection.

This collecting comes to me naturally. Almost unconsciously. It just happens. I think I inherited it from my father.

Here's an example: I saw an Archies lunch box at a flea market. I loved the Archies when I was a kid. So I bought it. A week later, I found a *Beverly Hillbillies* lunch box at a yard sale. I bought it. Two months later, I had a collection of thirty-seven lunch boxes.

I find something I like. I find another similar thing I like. And before you know it, I have another collection.

That's how this book came about.

I just started writing down some things that had happened in my life. Some funny things—at least to me. I wrote about my dad napping without underwear. I wrote about my mom giving me advice on what kind of underwear I should wear. I wrote about giving underwear as a gift to a six-year-old. I wrote about giving underwear to my wife. Before I knew it, I had another collection. A collection of underwear stories.

And as it always happens with my collecting, I wanted more. So, I started writing more stories. But not just about underwear. I wrote about talking shit. I wrote about taking shits. And leaving shits. And then I wrote about cussing. And cussing in songs. And why my favorite songs all have cussing in them.

I wrote about catching a bat. I wrote about jump-starting my car.

I wrote about living life without a microwave.

I wrote about what it's like to be a father. What it's like to be a son. What it's like to be a husband. What it's like to be me.

If someone asked what ties these stories together, what makes them a collection, I might say it's that they are relatively humorous. But I'd say the common thread is family.

It's all about family. And our family is quite a collection. A collection of talented, flawed, crazy, loveable characters. Real people who taught me many things, like that love and laughing can fix almost anything.

James Taylor wrote a song called "The Secret of Life." It was released when I was a kid, and at the time, I thought it was quite possibly the worst song ever written. Probably because there was no cussing in it. The only reason that it was on his album, I thought, was that he had writer's block and he needed something to fill two minutes and thirty-eight seconds so he could release the album. But forty years later, I realize that that song was the best song he ever released. Yes, better than "Carolina in My Mind." (I was born in North Carolina and went to the University of North Carolina, so you gotta know how much I love Carolina.) "The secret of life is enjoying the passage of time." Damn. That is so simple. And it's so true.

I really enjoy writing stories. I enjoy laughing and being silly and being around my family. (Most of the time.) I really hope you enjoy the time that you spend reading this book. 'Cause I'm really going to enjoy the money you spent buying it.

If you know me, or have spent any time with me, you may have heard a few of these stories. They're the kind of things that I talk about when I'm out for dinner. Or when I'm having a beer at Wooden Robot.

Now that I've written all these stories down, I realize that I have a dilemma. What am I going to talk about now when I go out?

"Did I tell you about the time I got a cement basketball court?"

"No, but I read it in your book."

"Did I tell you about the time Lucas used a fake ID in Vegas?"

"That's in your book too."

"Oh, right . . . Well, the weather is nice today . . ."

I'm gonna be the worst dinner guest ever.

So . . . maybe you're wondering how I came up with the title of this book?

I figured there was a good chance that my book could be a public failure and would become the subject of some cruel jokes. My book could actually become a punch line.

So I decided to go ahead and name the book after a punch line. "Nobody eats parsley." It's the punch line of one of my favorite jokes. One my Uncle Pete used to tell when I was a teenager. (No, I'm not going to tell you the joke now. You'll just have to keep reading.)

So now my book can never *become* a punch line, because it's always been a punch line.

There's a lot more of this convoluted type of thinking to follow.

I'm so happy to share this collection with you.

Enjoy.

P.S. As promised, here's a little more convoluted thinking: What's most amazing to me is that some of my collections become collectors themselves. This book, for example, will soon be sitting on your shelf, collecting dust.

PART I

DAVE'S WORLD

I was standing in line at the Circle K yesterday, and the guy behind the counter said, "I know you."

I smiled uncomfortably.

"You're that guy, that guy . . . I know you," he said, tapping his pen on the cash register.

Suddenly, I'm desperately trying to figure out how this guy knows me. Maybe he read my first book. *That's probably it*, I think. It's kinda cool to be a semicelebrity in Charlotte and be recognized in public.

Then it hits him. "Oh, I know . . . you're that guy from that old *Saturday Night Live* skit. Wayne's World . . . you're Garth!"

I quickly picked my ego off the floor, did my best air-drumsticks move, and said, "Party on, Wayne!"

"Party on, Garth!" he said, clapping his hands and laughing for a little longer than necessary.

Welcome to Dave's World.

JUMP START

O ur lawn looks like ass.

It's early March, and already our neighbor's yard looks like the eighteenth fairway at Augusta National. It's as green as a newly cut Christmas tree. Ours is brown and overrun with sweetgum balls and foot-tall onions. Certainly not yard-of-the-month material.

So even though it's 36 degrees and windy, I decide to mow the grass. I figure that at least the onions and dandelions will look presentable if they're all the same height. So I start the mower for the first time since October, and yes! It cranks on the first pull. I push the mower around the yard for about five minutes before it stops with an abrupt thump. I ran over a hidden stump and completely bent the blade. I did the same shit last March. Which means now my grass isn't getting cut, and I'm going to have to go see the marginally friendly folks at Park Seneca Lawnmower Repair again, who will tell me that it will be three weeks and ninety bucks to fix it. Good times.

So I wheel the broken mower back to the garage and decide to go see if I can borrow my neighbor Jim Doyle's mower. He says he's happy to let me use it and comes outside his house to show me how to start it. It's a brand-new, shiny Craftsman mower from Lowe's. Of course, it won't start. Jim pulled the starter cord probably fifty times. Nothing.

I suggest that maybe it has bad gas. I know a lot about bad gas. But that's another story. I learned from the lawn-mower repair people the last time that the kind of gas you use in a lawn mower can go bad over the winter and that you should buy new gas in the spring.

So we pour out the gas and I push the lawn mower over to our house. I fill it with the gas I have in my gas can. The mower still won't start. So, I pour all the gas out of the mower and the gas can and decide to go buy some really fresh gas.

I decide to drive my Acura TL, since I haven't driven it in about two weeks. But before I drive it, I need to pump up the tires. For some reason, they all seem to have slow leaks in them. So I grab the tire pump, aka the bike pump, to pump up the tires. Yes, I know it sounds strange, but a bike pump will inflate a car tire.

But first I need the pressure gauge to measure how much air pressure is in each tire. I can see by eyeballing it that the front passenger tire has about two pounds of pressure left in it. It should have thirty. I keep a tire gauge in the glove box, so I click the fob to unlock my car. It doesn't work. So I go old school and use the key to open the door.

I put the gas can in the passenger seat and sit down to start the car. The battery is dead. There are few things in life that I hate more than jump-starting a car, but now I've got to jump-start my fucking car so I can get one of two lame-ass lawn mowers to work.

I just want to mow the grass—and I don't even really want to do that.

I back my 4Runner up and start to attach the jumper cables to my Acura. But every time I jump-start a car, the same shit happens. I have total brain freeze and can't remember what cables go to what terminals, and which ones you connect first. I then do what most mechanically challenged people do: I take out my iPhone and I look up "jump-start car" images.

I find a diagram and then I start connecting them. Positive on the dead battery to positive on the booster battery. Then negative on the booster battery to a "ground" spot somewhere on the dead engine. I look around for the "ground" and can't find one. So, I grab the owner's manual out of the TL and look up jump-starting. It says to hook the last cable to a bolt near the fan belt, which will act as the "ground." I follow the instructions to a tee and attach the negative clamp to the "ground." The moment I do that, sparks fly and the horn on the dead car starts *honk! honk! honking!* like crazy. Like someone is breaking into it.

Fuck.

I quickly unhook the cables to get the horn to stop. Whew. *Damn, those Japanese horns are ear-piercing.* I have no idea what to do next, so I do what those people on *Who Wants to Be a Millionaire* do when they need a question answered. I phone a friend: my cousin Brad, who knows more about cars than Richard Petty. Brad laughs at me and says all I need to do is hook it up again, and when it starts honking again, use the key on the door and unlock it so that the car knows it isn't getting broken into.

So I look at my phone again to remember how to connect the cables again. This time when the horn begins honking, I stick the key in the door and the honking stops instantly. *Holy shit, Brad's a fucking genius.*

I finally get the car jump-started, and I remember that I need to pump up the front passenger tire. I grab the bike pump and quickly pump in just enough air to keep the wheel rim off the pavement. Then I drive to the gas station to get gas. I fill the can with premium gas. Normally, I buy regular, but damn it! I want that mower to start. I get back in my car and turn the ignition, and it's dead again.

So I have to ask someone to jump-start me at the gas station. Which is totally embarrassing. Once we do that and we get it started again, I drive over to the air pump to add some more air to my front tire. I leave the car running, of course. Can't risk my battery dying again. I inflate all four tires and go home with my gas.

I park the car in the driveway and leave it running. I damn sure don't want to have to look up how to jump-start it again. I fill the gas tank on the mower with the premium gas, and it cranks on the first try. Yes!

I decide to mow the grass before it gets dark. Forty-five minutes later, I finish mowing, and I take the mower back to Jim Doyle's house and have a beer with him to celebrate the fact that I got his mower to start.

When I walk back across the street to our house, I remember that I need to go to Advance Auto to get a new battery for the car. I walk back up to the car, which I left running before I mowed the grass. But now the car is off. *Damn it*, I thought, *Claire must have turned it off.* I hopped into the car and turned the ignition. Nothing. It's dead again.

I stormed into the house to confront my wife. Claire was sitting in the den watching an episode of *Chopped*. "Why did you turn my car off? I was trying to charge the battery."

"What are you talking about?"

"My car is dead again."

"Well, just jump-start it again and go get a new battery," she said.

I go back outside and go through the whole process all over again. I get the jumper cables out. I back the 4Runner beside the Acura. I start to hook the jumper cables up, and then I forget where they go, so I google jump-starting a car again. I start the booster car and then I get in the Acura and turn the key. But this time the horn doesn't blow. The engine doesn't start. Nothing happens.

Except for one thing: The lights on the dashboard come on. I can see the speedometer, the oil gauge, and one other very important instrument: the gas gauge. Which is sitting all the way on E.

It was out of gas.

And so was I.

THE POKER TABLE BET

Our family likes to bet. I guess it's the competition we enjoy. Or maybe it's just that we all love winning. Whatever the reason, the fact remains that Oakleys delight in gambling. My parents used to go to Atlantic City to play the slots. My younger sister, Lisa, who now runs the family business, rarely goes on a work trip without a stop at a local casino for a few hours of blackjack. I've been to Las Vegas thirty times now. None of them would qualify as a business trip. Unless you consider that my business . . . is winning.

Lisa and I realized a year or so ago that our mom, Pat, had never been to Las Vegas. Before my dad passed away, the two of them had visited casinos in Mississippi, Baltimore, and New Jersey, but she had never been to the mecca of gambling. Lisa and I decided that we would take Mom there to celebrate her seventy-seventh birthday in January.

We figured that a trip with her kids would give her something to look forward to and help get her through the chilly, dark months of December and January. We told her about our plan on Labor Day, after dinner at her house. She was thrilled. Then we told her the parameters for the trip that only a couple of fifty-something kids could concoct: We wanted *her* to pay for the trip—flights, hotel, food. And maybe even a little for gambling. We reasoned with her: Why hold on to your money to give us some inheritance when you could enjoy it *with* us?

Much to our surprise, she was still thrilled.

"Well, I've got a lot of frequent-flier miles from my credit card, so I guess I can book our flights with that," she said with a grin. "And don't you guys get some room nights comped sometimes? Rooms shouldn't be very expensive. OK, this sounds like fun. I'll pay for our food."

"Fantastic." Lisa and I hugged Mom and told her how much fun it was going to be.

"Don't forget about a little gambling money," I said.

"Well, we'll see about that."

The next five months flew by. The anticipation of our trip grew with each passing day. Every time I spoke with Mom on the phone, she was so excited. And every time, I prodded her about some gambling money.

"Well how much money are you thinking?" she finally asked.

"I don't know, maybe $10,000 each for you, me, and Lisa."

"$10,000? Are you out of your mind?!" she screeched.

"I'm just kidding, Mama." I chuckled to show her that it was a joke. "I was really thinking a thousand each?" I said, knowing full well that this was way more than she would ever think about giving us.

"$1000 each? Damn, you must be a high roller. Or just high." She laughed.

"I'm not either. I'm just thinking that we need to bring some cash."

"All right, I'll think about it."

Then I called Lisa and told her what I'd said. Lisa couldn't believe I'd asked for $1000 each.

"Doesn't hurt to ask," I said. "She knows I'm just messing with her."

I kept it up until the week before we left. Lisa called a couple of days before we were scheduled to leave and told me that Mom wasn't feeling very well. Lisa lives close by and checks in on her frequently. She said Mom had caught a cold and was coughing a lot. Mom was going to go to the doctor to get checked out and hopefully get some medication to knock this out so she'd be well enough to travel.

On the same call, Lisa told me that she and her sixteen-year-old daughter Emily liked playing Texas Hold'em so much that they were going to have a mother-daughter poker night in February. Emily had invited three of her girlfriends and their mothers to come over for a night of gambling. I loved hearing this, since I'd taught Emily how to play Texas Hold'em when we visited them for Thanksgiving.

"That is so cool," I said. "Do you have a poker table?"

"No, why?" Lisa said.

"Well, you can't host a poker tournament without a proper poker table."

"We're gonna play on the kitchen table."

"No, you can't. The cards will slide off the wood onto the floor. You need to be playing on felt."

"Well, how much does a poker table cost?"

"You can get one online from Amazon or Walmart for around $200. I've been looking for one for me, too. I want to host a game at my house."

"I'll look into it," Lisa said, "and I'll let you know what the doctor says about Mama."

The day before we were scheduled to leave, Lisa called and told me that the doctor had given Mom an antibiotic and prednisone to clear her breathing. But best of all, the doctor had given her the OK to fly to Vegas.

"Thank goodness," I said.

"We'll have to take it slow with her out there, but we're going," Lisa said. "And Mom is ready."

"Has she been to the bank?" I asked.

"I don't think so, but she said she's been putting away some cash for her gambling."

"For her gambling? What about our gambling?"

"David, you know she's not going to give us money for gambling. Not much, anyway."

"That's what you think," I said. "How much do you think she's going to give us?"

"I don't know . . . ," Lisa said, a touch of annoyance in her voice. "I just don't think that she has a lot of cash to give out."

"Well, she's going to give us something. I've been messing with her about it for the last five months."

"You want to bet on it?"

"Yeah, I do," I said. "We'll do an over-under bet."

For those of you who aren't obsessed with gambling like we are, an over-under bet is a wager where a number is set and you win based on whether the score is over or under the set number. This is used a lot in football games. Say the Panthers were playing the Packers. The over-under number for combined points the two teams would score in the game would be set by Vegas oddsmakers. Let's just say the over-under number for this game is 48. Let's say by some miracle the Panthers won the game 24–21. The total number of points is 45. This is less than 48. So, if you bet the under, you would win the wager.

"I'll let you set the number. Whatever number you pick, I'll take the over," I said.

"OK," Lisa said, "Let me see . . . How about $300? Mama will give us each $300."

"Perfect. I've got the over. You win if she gives us $300 or less, and I win if she gives us more than $300? Deal?"

"Deal."

"So what are we gonna to bet?" I asked.

"A poker table," Lisa said without hesitation.

"Oh my God, that's perfect." And we both lost it in hysterical laughter.

I saw Mom and Lisa the next day in the Charlotte airport. They had flown from Raleigh and we were flying to Vegas together. Mom looked beautiful and excited for an adventure. She had the same sparkle in her eyes that I picture her having on her very first visit to Charlotte in 1960. That was soon after she was crowned Miss Oxford in her hometown, and she traveled to the Queen City to participate in the Miss North Carolina pageant. She didn't win, but I always thought she should have. Lisa was dressed for Sin City success, wearing her lucky El Cortez Casino T-shirt and an impish grin on her face. She was psyched that I was there to talk with Mom, so she could concentrate on practicing her blackjack skills on her phone. Lisa was ready to win. I sat between them, the only time in my life I was ever happy to be in the middle seat. I was stoked for a great family bonding experience. And nothing bonds the Oakleys like gambling.

The flight was long, and I'm sure it was tough on my mom to sit in one place for that amount of time. But seeing the lights of Vegas when we touched down gave all of us a boost of energy. Lisa had arranged for a limo to pick us up and take us to the "Welcome to Las Vegas" sign. We got out, and the driver took a picture of us that was almost as iconic as the sign. Then we headed to the Bellagio, where we were staying. We had an early dinner and then Mom went to bed. She wanted to get some rest. "My gambling will start tomorrow, when I'm fresh."

The beginning of an unforgettable Vegas trip.

The next day after lunch, Mom was ready to pull the one-armed bandits. She said she had a feeling about "that machine," and pointed at a Wheel of Fortune slot machine that was located near the lobby of the Bellagio. I sat down at another Wheel of Fortune machine right beside hers, and Lisa, who had won $300 playing blackjack before lunch, started playing again at a table right beside the slot machine. I watched Mom play for about ten minutes and started to get bored. I decided to put some money in the machine where I was sitting. On my third play, my slot machine started playing loud, jangly music accompanied by a cacophony of beeps, bells, chimes and whistles. A deep prerecorded voice bellowed from the machine, "It's time to press again for the Gold Spin." So I did, and the electronic Wheel of Fortune spun round and round and came to a stop on 15X. Which meant that I got to spin the big wheel at the top of the machine, and whatever number it hit, I would win fifteen times that number.

"Mom, Lisa, come check this out!" and I pressed the Spin button. The large wheel spun and spun and slowed down and finally came to a stop on $100. We all started screaming like we had won a jackpot, because, well, we had won a jackpot. Fifteen times $100. $1500 to be exact! Man, this would be a trip never to be forgotten.

After our screaming and yelling had subsided a bit, Lisa walked over and said to me, "I just won the poker table for my house."

"What do you mean?"

"Mom just saw you win $1500. She's not giving you shit now." And we both cracked up.

Soon after, we went back up to the room to get ready for dinner and the show: the O show. Mom had always wanted to see a Cirque du Soleil show, and tonight we were going to see what I consider to be the best one. Honestly, I'm not a big fan of Cirque du Soleil, but O is the best of the ones I've seen. The best of the worst. I don't know, everyone seems to like them but me. I'd rather be gambling.

About thirty minutes into the show, my eyes were getting heavy and I was struggling to stay awake. Just as I was about to go into REM, Lisa hit me hard on the shoulder and said, "Get help. Something's wrong with Mom."

I looked at my mom, who was sitting between us in the darkened theater. She was out cold with her mouth wide open. It looked like she had just fallen asleep, but I could tell by Lisa's tone that she wasn't asleep. We tried to rouse her, but she was totally unconscious. I ran down the steps and grabbed an usher. "Call 911—my mom has had a heart attack. Or a stroke."

I ran into the lobby and told two other security people that this was an emergency and they needed to call the paramedics. I ran back into the theater and by then, there was a crowd around my mom. Mom was conscious again and talking with Lisa and another woman who was helping her. The paramedics arrived seconds later and helped carry her out of the theater into the lobby, while the acrobatic Cirque performers didn't miss a beat. Mom was totally lucid and said that she was really tired and was bored with the show, and had just wanted to go to sleep. They did a thorough exam on her and determined that she had fainted, perhaps because of a coughing fit. They took her blood pressure and it was a little low. My mom kept saying that all she needed was a little sleep.

"Please take me upstairs and put me to bed for the evening," Mom said.

"Well, it's your choice," one of the EMTs said, "but if it was my mom, I'd go to the ER just to make sure everything was OK."

So, much to my mom's chagrin, Lisa and I decided to take Mom to the ER.

Lisa rode with her in the ambulance. I followed in the first cab I could get. When I arrived, they were giving Mom liter after liter of fluids because she was dehydrated. They also were giving her medicine for her blood pressure, which was mysteriously dropping. They did a CT scan of her brain to see if there was a bleed. It was negative. After two hours of tests, her blood pressure continued to drop: 75/35 and falling. We could tell that the doctor was perplexed. He came and asked us again if she had fallen. The only explanation he seemed to have was that there might be some internal bleeding somewhere. But they had done scans of the brain and heart, and they showed nothing.

"Could her coughing attack have caused something to rupture?" Lisa asked.

"Noooo...," replied the doctor. Then he paused and said, "Maybe... maybe I need to get an abdominal CT scan."

He got the results back quickly. It showed that she was bleeding in her lower abdomen. "We need to get your Mom some blood. She's lost a lot. Hopefully we have A+ blood in the hospital."

He yelled at some nurses. "We have an hour—maybe an hour and a half—to make this work," he said. "Let's go!"

Lisa and I exchanged looks of disbelief. Was our mom going to die tonight? Had we pushed her too hard to come to Las Vegas? Had we really bet on how much money she was going to give us? We were total idiots.

Mom's condition was touch and go for the next three hours. Luckily, she took the transfusion well, and after it reached a low of 61/30, her blood pressure started to climb. By noon the next day, her condition had stabilized, and they moved her from the ER into the intensive care unit. She was conscious and in good spirits and very happy that we were there with her. She said she was just overtired.

Over the next five days, her condition slowly improved. On Wednesday, the doctors declared that miraculously, she was fit to travel home. After she was discharged, we decided to go back to the hotel for a night of rest before we attempted the long flight home. After a good night's sleep at the Bellagio, my mom woke up refreshed and feeling quite a bit better. She said she really wanted to pull the one-armed bandits before we went to the airport.

She was sitting in the chair by the window with a beautiful view of the Las Vegas strip when she looked at me and said something that made me very happy. "I have some money that I haven't had a chance to gamble with since I've been in the hospital, so I'm going to give you some, David."

She was holding two envelopes. She handed one to me. "This money is for you to gamble with tonight."

I smiled, thanked her profusely, and opened the envelope. Inside were three hundred-dollar bills.

"This is so nice, Mom. Do you think you have any more of those ones? Maybe one or two that I could add to this to tip the cocktail waitresses at the slot machines?"

"Oh, good idea. You can't tip them one of those big bills," she said as she handed me three singles.

"Thank you so much, Mom. I feel like I've already won big now." I gave her a hug.

Lisa was on the phone and gave me a look like, "I'm going to kill you, you cheating motherfucker." My shit-eating grin was ear to ear.

When Mom looked away, Lisa whispered to me, "The bet was that she gives both of us over three hundred bucks. She hasn't given me anything."

It took me less than a second to ask, "That was so nice of you to give me some cash, Mom, but what about Lisa? Do you have some greenbacks for your daughter?"

"Oh yes, I do." She handed Lisa another envelope with $400 in it.

I just couldn't stop smiling. I had just been handed $303, and more importantly, I had just won a poker table. Lisa couldn't help but laugh, because even after she bought a poker table for me, she was still up $200.

"Now that you two are in the money, let's go gamble," my mom said as she settled into her wheelchair. "Which one of you is going to push me? Let's go."

We gathered up all of Lisa and Mom's luggage and headed downstairs to the casino.

We had about twenty minutes to play the slots before we needed to get in the cab to the airport. I pushed Mom around the slots until she found the one that she felt was calling her. It was the Wheel of Fortune machine right next to the one that I had won on six days before. She put $20 in the machine, and on the third pull it started to make a racket. A wonderful racket. It was the same jangly music with beeps, bells, chimes, and whistles that I had heard a week earlier. The machine spoke again: "It's time to press again for the Gold Spin."

My mom pulled the lever, and the gold wheel started spinning. It spun and spun and spun, and it ground to a halt on 5X. Which meant that whatever number the big Wheel of Fortune wheel stopped on, my mom would win five times that amount.

She gathered her energy and breathed in as much oxygen as her poor lungs would let her. "Here we go," she said, and pressed the Spin button with the enthusiasm of someone who had just been released from prison rather than a hospital. The wheel spun round and round. We were all hypnotized with wonder, speculating on where it might stop. It clicked to a halt on $150, and my mom let out a yell that would've astonished her doctors. She had just won $750 on her way out of town. Which is the absolute best time to win, because you don't have time to bet your winnings on anything else.

As I rolled Mom's wheelchair through the lobby of the Bellagio on the way to the cab, I realized that we all were big winners on this trip. Mom won a slot jackpot, Lisa won big at blackjack, and I won a poker table. But none of our wins could compare to the biggest win ever in Vegas: Our mom made it home.

WHEN YA GOTTA GO, YA GOTTA GO

When asked, a lot of people will tell you that their favorite swear word is fuck. *Fuck* is pretty much the perfect word. It's a noun. It's a verb. An adjective. It's so versatile. Claire will tell you that it's her favorite. She even includes it as an interview question for potential employees at BooneOakley: "What's your favorite swear word?" An answer of *fuck* doesn't always result in that person being hired, but it pretty much guarantees a second interview.

I like the word *fuck*, but if I had to pick my favorite, I'd have to say *shit*. I've always been a shit talker. Not to be confused with a shit taker. I'm that too. But I've always wondered why it was called *taking a shit*. I've never taken a shit. If you took a shit, what would you do with it? You can't sell it on eBay. Well, maybe you could if you were famous. But who would do that? I don't take a shit. I leave a shit. Usually in the toilet.

A phrase that I love is *When ya gotta go, ya gotta go*. No truer statement has ever been made. Especially when it comes to leaving a shit. I'm sure you know what I'm talking about. It's that overwhelming signal that your lower intestine sends to your brain alerting your whole body that if you don't find a toilet pronto to release that Chipotle bean burrito you had for lunch, you're going to do something much worse than leave a shit. You're going to shit yourself.

That feeling has happened to me literally hundreds of times in my life. I don't remember all of them, but when you are going through it, all you can think about is swearing that you'll never eat shrimp lo mein from a food truck ever again. But once you find a toilet and evacuate, the sense of emergency subsides, and you go back to thinking about the important things in life, like why *shit* is such a great word.

Even though I don't remember each and every one of my *when ya gotta go* . . . incidents, there's one I'll never forget. I was in Las Vegas for March Madness, and after downing two appropriately named In-N-Out burgers for lunch, I got the urge to go. My mind told me immediately that this was going to happen pretty fast, so I quickly walked toward the men's room in the MGM Grand casino. As I got closer to the public restroom, the urge subsided a bit, and my mind, much like Google Maps, quickly recalculated my destination. *I think can make it to my room upstairs*, I told myself. I'm sure most people would agree that it's better to leave a shit in your hotel room than in the public toilet. Unless you are rooming with someone, and in that case it's better to leave a shit in the public restroom. That's just being considerate. And no, a courtesy flush and a can of Febreze is never enough to rid a hotel-room bathroom of the stench.

I got into the elevator and pressed the button to the sixteenth floor. As soon as the doors closed, I knew immediately that this was not a good plan. The urge to go was now stronger than ever. I pinched my ass as tightly as . . . well, as the last time I thought I was going to shit myself. On the twelfth floor, a mother and her young daughter got in. The door closed and the mom pressed the 14 button. The little girl whispered to her mom loud enough for me to hear her, "Mommy, it smells bad in here." The door opened and they quickly got out. I hit the 16 button again and finally the doors closed. I was almost there. The doors opened, and I started speed walking toward room 1623. But I had forgotten to calculate just how far my room was from the elevator. If you have ever stayed at the MGM Grand in Vegas, you know what I'm talking about. It's the largest hotel in the world, and the hallways are at least two miles long. Four miles if you urgently need to leave a shit.

But I kept walking. Walking with a mission. Walking like someone who had somewhere to go. Because I needed somewhere to go.

As I made my way down the hallway, I could see something in the distance. It was on the same side of the hall as my room. I assumed it was a room service cart that someone had left outside their door.

By this time, I had broken into a full-on sweat. I wasn't sure if it was the brisk walk, or the fact that every inch of my body was working overtime to prevent me from leaving a shit in the hallway.

When I was about a hundred feet away, I could see that it wasn't a room service cart. It was far worse. It was the maid's cart. And it was parked directly in front of Room 1623.

My door was open. The housekeeper said, "How are you sir?"

"Fine and thank you for cleaning," I said as I slammed the door shut, practically knocking her into the hallway.

I ran into the bathroom, got my pants off in the nick of time, sat down, and proceeded to blast that toilet like it had never been blasted before. An odor engulfed the room that was not in any way human. Unless it was the stench of rotting human. Most people will protest that their own shit doesn't stink, but this was so bad that I almost straight-up vomited.

Thank God I had remembered to turn on the exhaust fan when I ran in. Moments after the explosion, I carefully breathed a sigh of relief and thought to myself that maybe later that evening I'd raise a glass to the inventor of the bathroom exhaust fan, when I heard a familiar sound. It was the announcer from *The Price is Right*, saying "Dana, come on down! You're the next contestant on *The Price is Right!*" I took my eyes off the exhaust fan in the ceiling and saw I had left my bathroom door wide open. I figured I'd just left the TV on, until a strange figure appeared in the doorway: a second housekeeper, staring at me in disbelief. She motioned her hand back and forth in front of her nose and said in a thick accent, "I'm sorry you are not well, sir," and quickly scampered out of my room, gasping for air. She slammed the door behind her.

The moral of this story is that when ya gotta go, ya gotta go. Never pass up a perfectly good public restroom. It's the perfect place to leave a shit. In a public restroom, no one will ever know it was you.

THE BOOK SIGNING

One of the hardest things for me about writing a book is actually promoting my book. I think that's a common issue with most authors, but one might think that that wouldn't be a problem for me. After all, I'm an advertising guy. I'm always promoting stuff. But it's different when you're asked to promote your own writing. It's not a Bojangles' Cajun Filet Biscuit commercial. Or the latest Outer Banks campaign. It's a much more personal thing. It's saying, "Come look at me. Read my stories. Aren't I funny? Spend your money on me."

After writing *Why Is Your Name Upside Down?*, I had a big book-launch party at Old Mecklenburg Brewery in Charlotte. I invited a ton of folks. Much to my surprise, a ton of folks showed up. It's amazing how many people will brave a snowstorm for free beer. After getting them all liquored up, I actually sold a couple hundred books.

After that, I did a book signing at a local independent bookstore, Park Road Books. It's the best bookstore in Charlotte, and about fifty people came out to hear me talk about how great my book was. Truthfully, there were about a dozen people who came to see me, and the rest stopped in to get the February issue of *Organic Banking*. That evening, I sold forty-two books, if you include the six that my mom bought. I really appreciate everyone who bought one.

These two events pretty much exhausted my local friends-and-family network, so if I wanted to sell some more books, I knew I'd have to take the show on the road. That's right, it was time for a book tour! It's kind of like being in a rock band and going on tour. But instead of playing Madison Square Garden or the Hollywood Bowl, I was scheduled to appear in independent bookstores in Chapel Hill, Asheville, and Salisbury, North Carolina.

The one I was most excited about was the appearance at the South Main Book Company in Salisbury. By really excited, I mean scared shitless. I was scared shitless because the *Salisbury Post* had done an article on my book and publicized that I would be at the South Main Book Company on Friday evening from seven to eight thirty p.m. I wasn't scared because I thought a ton of people were going to show up. I was scared because I thought that one person would show up. One certain marketing director at Red Berry Tea, named Rob, who I had called out in the book as being the worst client that I had ever worked with.

Why did I agree to do it, then? Probably because I knew that Red Berry Tea's headquarters were in Salisbury, and somewhere deep down inside, I really wanted him to show up. You have to admit it would make a pretty good story if he did.

And if I was going to write a second book, I'd need something to write about, right?

The entire drive up I-85 to Salisbury, all I could think about was Rob showing up to buy a book. What would he be wearing? Would he come straight from work? Or would he stop by Pistol Pop's Firearms on the way? Then I would talk myself out of that notion and convince myself that he would never show up because he'd be too embarrassed for anyone to know that I had called him out. Plus, he'd never acknowledge me, or that I had gotten the better of him, by showing up. Then my thoughts would go another way. What if this fucker is a madman, and me calling him out sent him over the edge? That dude could very well show up with an AK-47 and blow me away. This was the thought that I really couldn't get out of my mind.

It kept getting worse the closer I got to Salisbury. Maybe it wouldn't be an assault rifle. Maybe he would sneak up behind me and clock me over the head with a bottle of Red Berry Tea, then cut my throat with the broken bottle.

By the time I got to the bookstore, I was a paranoid, shivering mess. I introduced myself to Delores, the owner, and she asked if I was feeling all right. I told her that I was OK, just thirsty. She said it was nice to meet me and went to get me a glass of water. When she came back, she said she was so happy that the *Salisbury Post* had written such a glowing review of the book. She was sure that there would be a lot of interest in my writing.

Delores reached behind the counter and pulled out a card table and opened it. "Here you go," she said, "You can set up right over there." I unfolded a folding chair and set it behind the table and unpacked my box of books. I'd brought twenty inside with me but had more in my car in case we needed them.

I quickly cased the bookstore to make sure my killer wasn't there. I looked up and down every aisle, but there was no sign of Rob. I even checked the bathroom, just to be safe. At the allotted time for the signing, I sat down in the folding chair behind the card table and started waiting for my adoring fans to show up.

I'd never really noticed before how quiet a bookstore can be. It's so different from a library. There's always a low rustling sound in a library. Not that I've spent a lot of time in libraries. Even in college, I only went to the library the night before exams to pretend like I was studying. But every single time I've been in a library—OK, both times—there were people there. And that was the main difference. There wasn't a soul in this bookstore. Except for me. Even Delores was nowhere to be seen.

A half hour later, the front door finally opened, and the first customers of the evening walked in—a woman and a small boy. They walked around looking at books for a while, and when they finally couldn't ignore me anymore, the mom said to the son, "Look Bobby, this man is like you, and he wrote a book about it."

She smiled at me and then her son walked over. "He sees things upside down just like you. He has dyslexia too."

I just smiled and nodded.

"Is your book about how you overcame your disability to become successful?" she asked.

I nodded again, smiled and said, "You can do anything if you stay in school and work really hard."

"See, Bobby, maybe we should buy this man's book."

I was thinking, *Please don't buy this book, there's a chapter about dogs fucking in it.* (In my first book, I wrote about how I came up with a big television commercial idea for the Humane Society. It's not a story for small children. But if you haven't heard it, please order the book immediately. You may regret the purchase, but I'm sure you've wasted money before.)

She picked up one of my books and looked closely at the cover and then said, "C'mon, Bobby let's go. We gotta get you a haircut," and they walked out the door.

By this time, I was actually hoping that Rob would show up with his AK-47 and kill me, just to put me out of my misery. But I wasn't that lucky. I sat there for another forty-five minutes, and no one else came in the store. Not a single person.

Finally, Delores came over and apologized to me. "I'm so sorry, David, I've never seen it so slow in here."

"That's OK," I said as I packed my twenty books back into the cardboard box. "At least I didn't get killed."

"Get killed?"

"Oh, yeah, I just had this weird thought that the marketing director from Red Berry Tea would come in here and murder me."

"Why would he do that?"

"Because in my book, I wrote that he was the worst client in history."

"Well, lucky for you, I guess he hasn't read your book."

Hasn't read my book, I thought? It had never occurred to me that he hadn't read my book. When I wrote the chapter about Rob, I knew that it would upset him. I wanted to expose him for being the talentless, sadistic douche of a client that he was. Heck, that's what drove me to write the darn story. The whole time I was writing it, I imagined Rob's eyes widening in rage when he read my words that shouted to the whole world that he was an idiot. The chapter was designed to get back at him for all the pain and suffering he had imposed on our ad agency. It was going to be sweet revenge. Perfectly timed to be delivered when Rob was least expecting it. I'd always heard that revenge is best served cold. But apparently, it hadn't been served at all.

Then I asked Delores a question that as soon as it came off my tongue, I knew I shouldn't have asked.

"Did you enjoy it?"

"Well," she said, "honestly, I haven't read it either."

OK, this evening was getting better by the minute. Not only had Rob not read it, but the owner of the bookstore hadn't read it. The owner who'd invited me to do a book signing at her store. As I walked down the street to my car, carrying my box of books, I remembered she hadn't actually invited me. I'd invited myself. I was out to promote my book and more importantly to sell some books. But how many books had I sold that evening? Zero. Nada. Zilch. I had been shut out. This evening was turning out to be the one of the most humbling, humiliating experiences of my life.

For an insecure writer, there's nothing like the realization that no one really cares that you wrote a book. As I drove back to Charlotte, I couldn't get that thought out of my head. *No one really cares that I wrote a book.*

But people would have cared if Rob had come into the bookstore and killed me. I would have sold a ton of books. Not that night, though, because the store would have been a crime scene.

I could just see the headlines in the press: "Author slain in bookstore. Former client charged with murder! Defendant claims Oakley slandered him, pleads insanity."

Once the story hit the press, *Why Is Your Name Upside Down?* would have sold like hotcakes. It would have been a *New York Times* bestseller.

But if that had happened, I wouldn't have been able to enjoy the financial windfall. I would be dead. I also wouldn't have been able to write this second book, which you bought. I guess I must be getting better at self-promotion.

Thank you for your purchase.

MY PLEASURE

Let's say its lunchtime and you're hungry. You don't have a lot of time before you have to be back at work. You see two fast food restaurants ahead on the right side of the road. The drive-thru line of one has two cars, and the other one has twenty. Which one do you choose? The one with just two cars in line, right? Wrong. If the one with twenty cars in line is Chick-fil-A, you choose Chick-fil-A.

Chick-fil-A is consistently one of the most efficient restaurant drive-thru operations I have ever seen. They keep the line moving and deliver your food with smiles on their faces and "my pleasure" on their lips. Great service has become commonplace for them. They've set the bar so high for themselves that they have to do exceptional things to stand out. That's just what I experienced on my most recent visit.

My daughter Sydney, our accounting director Katy Spiecha, and I were on our way back from a client meeting last week, and we needed to grab a bite to eat. We had another meeting at BooneOakley in thirty minutes, so we needed to be quick. We saw a Burger King with two cars in the drive-thru and a Chick-fil-A, which had a line of at least twenty. Obviously, we chose Chick-fil-A.

We took our place in line. Within a minute, we pulled up beside a smiling young lady in a Chick-fil-A uniform with some sort of tablet in her hand. I put the window down and she said, "Welcome to Chick-fil-A. Can I take your order?"

"You certainly can," I replied, and reflected on how nice it was to give my order to a real person instead of one of those staticky intercom systems that most fast food places have. "These two young ladies with me will order first. Katy?"

Katy was in the passenger seat and leaned toward my window. "Hi, I'd like to get a Chick-fil-A Sandwich with a side of fries and a water."

Then Sydney put the rear window down and asked, "Could I have a number-one combo with fries and a regular unsweetened tea?"

"Yes, thank you," replied the young lady. She then looked at me and asked, "And what would you like today, sir?"

"I'm not going to have anything here today. I'm going to get my lunch at Bojangles," I said with a straight face.

"Really?" she asked, kind of taken aback but still smiling.

Then I started laughing. "No, I'm just messing with you. I'd like to have a number-one combo with fries and a large unsweetened iced tea. And extra pickles on the sandwich."

"OK, sir, I've got your order. The total will be $22.74. How would you like to pay today?"

As I was reaching for my credit card, I said, "Actually, I'd like *you* to pay for it today."

"You want me to pay for it?" she said and adjusted the brim of her cap. "Well, let me see . . ." She looked at her iPad and started pressing a bunch of things on it. By this time, I had found my credit card was holding it out the window. She looked up from her iPad and saw me handing her my credit card.

"Oh no, sir, that won't be necessary today. This one's on me."

"Wait, what?" Now I was the one who was totally taken aback and confused. "What do you mean you're paying for it? I was just joking around."

"Our manager lets us pick a few people every day to give a free lunch. I chose you today. We call it our 'random act of lunch.'"

I couldn't believe it. Once again, Chick-fil-A had totally outdone themselves. It's all about customer service. When I got back to the office, I told everyone there about it. And now I'm telling you about it.

It reminded me of how my dad ran things at Cedar Creek Pottery when I was growing up. If he liked someone, occasionally, he'd give them a pot for free. If a customer ever returned a piece of pottery they'd bought, he'd give them their money back. No questions asked.

I thought this was a strange policy and asked him about it. "Why don't you ask for a receipt when someone returns something? If I bought something at Waccamaw Pottery in Myrtle Beach and wanted to return it, I'd have to have a receipt to get my money back."

"Well, first of all, we're not Waccamaw Pottery," he said. "If you trust people and treat them right, with respect, they'll come back. And you know what customers do when they come back? They buy more."

It made sense forty years ago, and it still makes sense today. Chick-fil-A totally gets it. But not everyone does.

A week later, Claire and I spent a relaxing weekend of boating, swimming, and soaking up the sun in Destin, Florida. Before we flew home, we decided to stop at Destin Commons Mall. We still had three hours before our flight took off, so what better time to shop for a new bathing suit? Never mind that we were leaving Destin. Who buys a bathing suit on the way home from the beach? Apparently, we do.

We went into a surf shop called Maui Nix and started looking around. I wanted a pair of board shorts and asked the manager where I would find them. He was typing something on his computer and didn't even look up when he said, "They're all over the store, mostly in that direction," and vaguely pointed toward the area of the store near the door where I'd just walked in.

"OK, thanks," I said, and turned and looked around. Claire and I scoured the racks, and we found three pairs of shorts that I liked. I asked the manager if I could try them on. "Yes, the fitting room's in the back," he said, again without even looking at me.

I tried them on individually and decided that I liked one of them well enough to buy them. By this time, Claire was trying on flip-flops. "I'm going to go to the bathroom while you look at those," I said to Claire. I then looked around the store for the bathroom. I didn't see one. I saw a young lady folding towels and I asked her where the restroom was. She said they didn't have a public restroom.

"Well, do you have a private one?" I asked.

"Yes, we do," she said.

"Well, can I use it?" I asked.

"It's OK with me, but you'll have to ask my boss."

She pointed at the guy at the counter, who I have already met. I walked up to him and said, "Do you mind if I use your bathroom?" Now, I figured that wasn't a whole lot to ask since I was buying a pair of $75 board shorts.

"I'm sorry, sir, we don't have a public restroom. There's one at Bass Pro Shop."

I had to pee pretty bad, so I took off in search of the Bass Pro Shop.

I'd never been to this Bass Pro Shop before. It was gigantic. There were boats and fish tanks and camouflage shit everywhere. There was so much visual stimuli, I almost forgot why I was there. Then I saw a salesman and asked where the restroom was. "Our regular restrooms are upstairs," he said, and pointed up the stairs where I could see a sign that said Restrooms. "But our really nice restrooms are in the boat room. It's a little farther to walk, but they're individual restrooms and they are a lot nicer."

"Well, thank you. I really appreciate your help," I said. I went to the nice restroom and did my business.

On the way out of that nice Bass Pro Shop restroom, something immediately caught my eye. It was a large rack of board shorts. And hanging on the rack was the exact same pair of shorts that I'd liked at Maui Nix. So I bought them.

I walked back to Maui Nix, and Claire was at the counter about to pay for the board shorts we had selected earlier. "Where have you been?" she asked.

"I went to Bass Pro Shop to use the bathroom."

I looked at the manager, who was ringing up the sale and said, "You were right, they do have a bathroom at Bass Pro Shop. It's really nice. And you know what else? They have really cool board shorts."

I reached into my Bass Pro Shop bag and pulled out the shorts. "So I bought a pair. Aren't they nice?" This time he actually looked at me. "Thank you so much for your help, sir. I never would have found them without you."

Claire and I walked out of the store.

I'm sure that manager really didn't care that I hadn't bought my board shorts there. And I'll never go back.

When customers don't come back, you know what they buy?

Nothing.

Chick-fil-A knows you can always go somewhere else. They just make sure you don't even think about it.

MY TATTOO

Every once in a while, I get asked the question, "Do you have a tattoo?"

I often think about getting one. Not because I really want a tattoo, but because I wonder if there is anything I feel strongly enough about to have it permanently branded on my body.

You have to believe in your tattoo so passionately that you will have no regrets. If you don't know what I'm talking about, google tattoo mistakes. That's where I found a remarkable tattoo on a guy's forearm. It looked great. Except for one thing. *No Regrets* was spelled, *No Regerts*. Everyone thinks his tattoo artist royally screwed up, and that the guy was a total moron, but I believe the guy did it on purpose, to demonstrate the message his tattoo aims to convey: He doesn't look back. What's done is done. He's always moving forward. He has no regerts. This guy is a tattoo genius.

If I get a tattoo, I want to feel as proud of my tattoo as that guy feels about his. So, what do I believe in? I love Claire, and a tattoo of her on my bicep could be nice. But I can't imagine any tattoo artist ever capturing her beauty on my arm. Plus, I'm convinced they would never get her hair right.

I'm infatuated with Las Vegas. OK, I'm obsessed with Las Vegas. I have thought long and hard about getting the famous "Welcome to Las Vegas" sign tattooed on my shoulder. I've also considered getting the four suits of cards: a red heart, black spade, red diamond, and black club in a row etched on my forearm.

I'm also very indecisive, in case you haven't noticed.

I've considered Wile E. Coyote. He's been my favorite *Looney Tunes* character ever since I got him on a Hardee's glass back in middle school. I've even toyed with the idea of getting a Pokémon tattoo. I'm way into the Pokémon Go game and play it on my iPhone every day. There's no question that if I got a Pokémon character, it would be Snorlax. I'm probably the only person on earth who snores as much as him, and he kinda looks me.

That was my dream tat of choice until today. I was walking on the boardwalk in Destin, Florida, where having a tattoo or multiple tattoos apparently is a requirement to be allowed to breathe. Today, I've seen so many folks who have multiple tattoos that I'm shocked when someone walks by without one. One thing's for sure: these folks clearly couldn't have put too much thought into their tattoos. There's no way someone with twenty-seven tats on their back—I counted— could have a real reason for each and every one. Shit, they probably hadn't even seen some of them. Clearly, I'm overthinking this whole idea of having to justify getting a tattoo.

As I walked by the fishing boats, I decided, why not just get a fish tattoo? I love sushi. I love fishing. Fish are cool. But what fish would make the best body art on me? Is there a Pokémon fish? Yes. Magikarp. That would be pretty dope, but Magikarp looks like a flopping drunken goldfish, so you'd have to be into Pokémon to know what it was. Hmmm . . . maybe a whale, since I'm a whale in Vegas. No, that's not really true. Then it hit me. A tuna. A tuna is a fish. Tuna is my favorite sushi. I'm going to get a tuna. Then when anyone asks me what kind of fish is on my arm, I'll tell them it's my tat-tuna!!! Decision made!

Not only is it a great tat idea, it's the best dad joke ever. Tat-tuna. OMG, I crack myself up.

The problem now is that I'm obsessive. I know that once I get started with one tattoo, I won't stop. My obsessive side will take over. After waiting fifty-seven years to get my first tat-tuna, I'm afraid that I'd be getting a second one within fifty-seven days. I know it would be the heart, spade, diamond, club tattoo. Fifty-seven hours or so later, I'd be back getting ink again.

By the end of the week, I'd probably be appearing on Ink Masters as a human canvas, letting the contestants tattoo a donkey humping a porcupine on my left butt cheek.

Soon thereafter, I'd get a beautiful, intricately designed tat on my lower back. A tramp stamp. But it wouldn't just be a random tramp stamp design; the tat would actually spell out *Tramp Stamp* in Times New Roman, so there would be no question what it was.

After that I'd probably get a tat a day for a year, until every square inch of my body was covered in ink.

So, to answer the question, no, I don't have a tattoo.

Yet.

THE UFO UPSTAIRS

We've all heard tales about folks seeing UFOs. Usually it happens in a tall cornfield on a moonlit night, or on some deserted stretch of highway in the middle of the Badlands of South Dakota. Looking up in the night sky and seeing a flying saucer hovering above you is no doubt very scary. But that doesn't come close to the sheer terror you feel when you see a UFO in your house. That's right. I had a close encounter of the third kind with an unidentified flying object in my own home.

It was Sunday evening, July 21, 2019. It had been a long, hot, and humid North Carolina weekend. We had hosted Claire's mom for dinner, and Claire had just left to take her back home. I was ready to relax and watch some TV, but I remembered that I had to fly out of town the next morning for work, so I decided I'd better pack. We keep our suitcases upstairs in the closet in Sydney's old bedroom, so I went up the steps and opened the door. It was pitch-black and extremely hot because our HVAC system does a less-than-adequate job cooling the upstairs, but we don't care because no one sleeps up there anymore now that Sydney has her own apartment. I reached around and flipped the light switch, and out of nowhere it came at me. Straight for my face. The UFO changed direction in a split second and flew right by my head, brushing my hair.

I screamed like a six-year-old girl seeing her first daddy longlegs. I had no idea my voice could reach the octaves of Celine Dion. Nor did I know that I could turn off the lights, slam the door, and descend a flight of stairs all in less than one second. But I did. Whatever it was, it scared every ounce of masculinity right out of me. That shit was terrifying. My heart was beating like Charlie Watts, and I was breathing like a chain smoker after running a hundred-yard dash. This mystery flying mini-monster had grazed me and now was in control of the upper extremities of our home. I tried to catch my breath. *What am I going to do?* I thought. *I know, I'll just leave the upstairs door closed and go back in the morning.* But I needed my suitcase. Damn it. Traveling for work is always a pain in the ass.

OK, calm down, David, calm down. What was that thing that came after me? Was it a bird? We had had grackles that nested in our attic a few years back. Maybe it was a lost chickadee, a sweet little bird that somehow came in the back door when the dog was outside. But this thing flew in a really erratic pattern. *Maybe, please no, just maybe, please no, could it be a rat with wings? Otherwise known as a bat. Oh, please don't let it be a bat.*

I've always been a fan of Batman. In fact, my first birthday party, when I was six, was a Batman party. My mom made handmade invites in the shape of Bruce Wayne's Batman symbol, and all my friends came over. But I don't like real bats. I'm not afraid of many other wild animals, insects, or bugs. I'm from what Claire affectionately calls "the Wild Kingdom." I grew up catching grasshoppers and digging fishing worms to go fishing. I'd catch frogs and toads. I have no issue smashing a black widow spider with my fingers. It just doesn't bother me. Last summer I was in our kitchen making a turkey sandwich and I looked down, and there about two inches from my bare feet was a foot-long copperhead. I didn't think twice about it. I just backed away slowly and opened a drawer behind me and got an oven mitt. I put it on, bent down and grabbed the snake behind the head, took him outside to the driveway, and promptly chopped his head off with a garden hoe.

But bats . . . that's another story. I thought that UFO might be a bat. Damn. I had no idea what to do about it. So, I did what I normally do when I don't know what to do. I got my laptop and googled it. I googled how to catch a bat in your house. If I was scared before, I was petrified after reading it. Bats can be rabid. Especially bats that get in your house. They don't want to be in your house. They are crazy bats. You've heard of being bat-shit crazy? That's from the kind of rabies-spreading bats that get into your house.

With each paragraph I read, my anxiety level rose exponentially. If a bat bites or scratches you, you must immediately go to the emergency room. If there is only one bat, odds are it's rabid. But you never know: if one bat is there, you may have hundreds more in the wall. Shit, this was way, way, way worse than being in the middle of nowhere looking at a flying saucer spinning its way toward you.

I needed to change my google search to something more practical. Like how to catch a flying rat, I mean bat in your house. Of course, I got served up an ad: *Call Critter Control*. Of course, that was logical, but it was almost eleven on a Sunday night. I'd be better served to call panic-attack control now. OK, here was something: "To catch a bat, all you need is nerve and a coffee can." I didn't have either. Who buys coffee in a can these days? I haven't seen a can of coffee since Reagan was president. Maybe we had something that was kind of like a coffee can? I started looking around the kitchen. A Tupperware bowl? No, too big. Maybe the pot I brew tea in would work? No, the handle makes it too cumbersome. I went into our pantry and saw something that just might work: a large can of mixed nuts that someone gave us for Christmas. It looked just like a coffee can, except that it had pictures of nuts on the side. Maybe this would confuse the bat, who might have heard that people sometimes use coffee cans as a trap.

I opened the can of nuts and poured them into a big pottery bowl. The instructions on how to catch the bat are simple: wait until the bat is roosting and sneak up on him. But what if it's a female bat? I sure hoped this worked for both sexes. "Sneak up on the bat and put the coffee can over him. Then slide the top of the can between the wall and the can and seal him up." Simple as that. *OK, I think I can do it.*

All I needed now was a little courage. That and a little coverage. No, I needed maximum coverage. There was no way I was going back up those stairs barefooted, wearing a T-shirt and shorts. I might not catch this fucker, but I damn sure was not going to let him give me rabies. So I decided to put together my bat battle suit. I grabbed a pair of ski pants and put on my hiking boots. I dug out my black North Face jacket from the back of the closet and put it on over my T-shirt and zipped it up tight around my neck. I tied a bandanna around my neck to make sure as little skin as possible was exposed. I tied my hair in a ponytail and stuffed it under my Panthers baseball cap, which I wore backward, so the interloper wouldn't get caught in my hair.

Now all I needed were gloves. *Oven mitts will work*, I thought. I went back to the kitchen and tried them on, but they were too bulky to hold the nut can. I remembered Johnny Cochran in the O. J. Simpson trial saying something like, "If the mitt don't fit, you gonna get bit." I had to think of something else. *Wait. I got it.* The gloves Aunt Hallie gave me three years ago for pruning roses that I had never used. Perfect. If thorns couldn't get you with these gloves, neither could little bat fangs. If these elbow-length gloves had been blue, they would have looked exactly like what Batman wore. And of course, I put on my glasses, because to catch a bat you can't have bat-like vision.

OK, now I was dressed for success. The only thing holding me back was fear of that motherfucker. And the fact that wearing all this shit was hotter than my sister's glass-blowing furnace. I took a couple of deep breaths and started to climb the steps to Sydney's bedroom. I slowly opened the door. OK, good. Nothing is flying at me this time. I flipped on the light for one second and quickly turned it back off. I didn't see anything. I closed the door fast and stepped back out into the hallway again. I have no idea why I did this; it just seemed like the right thing to do. I guess I wasn't quite ready. I took a deep breath and gathered myself to try again. I opened the door and flipped the light switch. This time I left the light on. I looked around the room and I saw it. It was no longer a UFO. It was definitely a bat. He or she was hanging upside down on the other side of the room at the top of the window. I was so happy he was hanging. Much better than flying wildly at me.

I slowly walked across the room toward the culprit. The problem is that he was hanging upside down between the window and the window blinds. I crept toward the winged one, and with each step, more sweat dripped off my brow. I realized that my plan of trapping this bugger in the nut can would not work, because the blinds are not a flat surface. My only hope was that he was fast asleep, and I could slowly close the blinds until they were flat, and I could put the mixed nuts can on top of him then. So I started slowly turning the thingamajig that closes the blinds. Very slowly. Very, very, slowly. *It's almost flat; this is working just like I planned,* and then, *Oh shit, oh shit, oh shit!!!*

The bat was not hanging anymore; he was ready to do some fanging. He wildly flew to the other side of the room and then turned around and flew directly back toward me. Or as directly as a bat can fly. He was going all over the fucking place. Up and down and from side to side, and *he's coming straight for my face—no, he's flying back toward the bathroom—now he's heading over to the ceiling fan. Now he's going back toward the window and then a sharp right turn and straight toward my eyes. He's coming straight to attack my nose. The damn mixed-nut can can't help me now!*

Instinct took over, and the pruning gloves led the way. With catlike quickness—which is faster than bat quickness, by the way—I took a swipe at him and knocked him straight to the carpet. I continued my feline attack and pounced on the squeaking varmint. I slammed the open end of the mixed-nut can down on top of him. I heard him fluttering around inside. I looked around the room for the lid of the can. I stretched to reach it and quickly slid the top between the can and the carpet. *I got him! I got him! I got him! Yesssssss!!!!*

I lay there on the floor, drenched in sweat, clenching the mixed-nut can, and breathed a giant sigh of relief. I closed my eyes and immediately saw a triumphant Freddie Mercury on stage at Live Aid. I jumped to my feet in a super adrenaline rush–induced celebration, and at the top of my lungs I started singing as I strutted around the room: "I am the champion my friend, I'll keep on bat-catching till the end. I am the bat-catching champion of the world."

Then I heard the bat squeaking inside the can. I had to release him before he suffocated. I gathered myself and walked downstairs with my captive in hand. I went outside and put the can down on the porch. I opened the top of the can and quickly backed about ten feet away. Nothing happened. The bat stayed in the can. I thought that maybe he was hurt, and I felt a gnawing sense of guilt that I was too rough catching him, or maybe I'd shaken him too hard during my impromptu Queen performance.

I walked closer to the can to see if he was OK. The bat climbed to the top of the can and jumped out onto the porch. He fluttered his wings for a moment and then flew out into the night, never to be seen again. Until a few seconds later, when he swooped down out of nowhere and went straight for my head again. I ducked and screamed again, but not as loudly as before.

Because he was no longer a UFO. I had identified him. He was a bat.

BILLIE JEAN

You'd think that by the time you're in your fifties you would've experienced almost everything. But let me tell you, there are a lot of firsts after you turn fifty. Like your first letter from AARP, your first gray pubic hair, and of course, your first colonoscopy.

I was a little apprehensive when I went into have my colonoscopy. But after taking the super-soaker laxative that made me pee out of my ass all night long the night before, I wasn't afraid of anything. I was ready to go in and get it over with.

As I stretched out on the operating table, the nurse said to me, "We're going to give you this propofol, and you're going to fall into a nice little slumber."

"That's the drug made famous by Michael Jackson, right?"

"Yes, I think you're right," the nurse said as she turned the switch on the IV drip. "I'm starting the propofol now, so you should be sleeping in just a few seconds."

"OK."

I wondered if Michael Jackson had turned fifty and gone in for his colonoscopy and had a hit of propofol and said to himself, "This shit is good. I'm going to get my doctor to give me some of this stuff to help me sleep every night."

The next thing I knew I was waking up. I was a little groggy, but man, I felt good. It was like I'd slept for ten hours. And I had no recollection of anyone poking and prodding up my butt. I thought, *This shit is good. I'm going to get my doctor to give me some of this stuff to help me sleep every night.*

"Hi, David," the nurse said. "We're all done. How do you feel?"

"I feel great."

"Oh good. You may feel a little bloated now, and that's normal."

"I do."

"You may feel the urge to pass some gas, and that's normal. It's OK for you to pass gas now."

"Wow, no one has ever said that to me before."

"Yes, we pumped air into your intestines so the camera could look around. It's only natural that the air needs to come out. So, feel free to let it out."

"OK," I said hesitantly.

I turned over on my side and lifted my leg slightly. I let out a loud gust of wind that sounded like an air horn and lasted no less than five seconds. It was quickly followed by several shorter bursts of flatulence that sounded not unlike an overconfident third-chair middle school trombonist.

I looked over at the nurse, who acted like she didn't even notice. I ripped another and she didn't even bat an eye.

"Ummm . . . I have to ask you something. Does everyone break wind like this after a colonoscopy?

"Yes."

"How do you stand it?" I said, giggling.

"You get used to it." She shrugged.

"I don't know how anyone gets used to that," I said. I cut another one.

"Well, it's part of the job, and they don't smell. There's nothing in your intestines right now that could smell bad."

"Well, that's true. I think I probably shit out several organs last night," I said, then laughed.

The nurse didn't crack a smile and went back to typing on her laptop.

"So, let me ask you one more thing. Farts really don't bother you in here?"

"No."

"What about in real life? What if someone farts beside you in a movie theater, for instance?"

"Well, that's gross."

"OK, that's what I thought. I was just checking. What about Michael Jackson?"

"What about him?"

"I was just wondering after he had his colonoscopy, did Michael Jackson fart just like me?

"I wasn't with Michael Jackson when he had his colonoscopy. But I'm sure he passed gas just like everyone else."

I lay there staring at the ceiling tiles for a moment, lifted my leg and let out one more significant gust of wind. I thought, *There's no way Michael Jackson ripped them like me. He probably farted to the tune of "Billie Jean." Or maybe "Thriller."*

THE MONEY BOX

I love cash. All kinds. Johnny Cash. Rosanne Cash. But more than any other form of cash, I love cash dollars.

It all started when I was a kid.

Once after I had finished mowing the grass, my dad asked me if I'd like to be paid with an old ten or a new one. I said I'll take a new one. And he handed me a crisp one-dollar bill. Then he busted out laughing. Only after laughing for what seemed to me like two hours did he give me the other nine one-dollar bills.

My Grandma Jenny had a money jar. It was a half-gallon jar that she kept in her closet. It was her rainy-day fund. When she had some spare change, she dropped it into the jar. I was fascinated by her money jar. It was a big jar, and it was about three-quarters full of quarters, dimes, nickels, and an occasional fifty-cent piece. She didn't put pennies in it. Only silver coins. Anyway, it was the most money that I'd ever seen. I hoped that someday I would have a big money jar of my own.

Well, forty years later, I have one. Except it's not a money jar. It's a money box. It's a money box because I don't collect coins. I collect dollar bills. It started a few years ago at a Carolina Panthers football game. I bought a Budweiser for $11. Budweiser is the King of Beers, so I understand having to pay a premium for something so delicious, but $11 still seemed a little steep. But it was hot, I was thirsty, and the Bud was cold. I handed the beer lady a twenty. She gave me a five and four ones in change. I gave her a dollar tip, and I stuffed the rest in my pocket and went to my seat to watch the game. This must have happened a few more times that afternoon, because when I got home, I had eighteen one-dollar bills. I didn't want to walk around all day at work on Monday with eighteen dollar bills in my pocket, because they're kinda bulky, and my pants were already kinda tight from drinking beer all day at the Panthers game. So, I put the singles in the bottom of my sock drawer.

Over the next couple of months, every time I got a dollar bill in change, I kept it and put it in my sock drawer. Before I knew it, I had a nice stack of dollar bills. One Saturday morning, I decided to count them. I had 122. Then I did what any normal guy would do with 122 one-dollar bills. I went straight to the Uptown Cabaret, Charlotte's premier gentlemen's club. OK, I didn't do that, but I did consider it. Instead, I counted out a hundred ones, grabbed a ponytail holder, and wrapped it around the stack. I put the remaining twenty-two bills back in my sock drawer, and I put the stack of one hundred bills into an empty Steve Madden shoe box. That's my money box.

I continued putting my extra one-dollar bills in my sock drawer. Every few months I counted them, and if I had a hundred dollar bills, I would get a ponytail holder and wrap it around the stack. Then I'd put it in my money box.

This went on for a little while. A little while if you consider several years a little while. One morning, I opened my sock drawer and it looked like I had over a hundred ones there. So I did what I normally did. I counted out a hundred ones and got a ponytail holder and wrapped it around them. Then I put that stack of $100 into my money box. But this time it was different. When I put this hundred in, there was no room for any more money. This time, the money box was full.

Wow, I thought. Grandma Jenny would be proud. I had a whole shoebox full of cash. I counted the stacks of ones, and to my surprise, I had thirty-six ponytail-holder-wrapped stacks, each containing $100. Wow. $3600. That's a lot of cash.

At this point I realized that I was kind of fucked. How am I ever going to be able to cash in this money? I can't exactly go to the bank with a money box full of $3600 in one-dollar bills. They're going think I either ripped off a bunch of vending machines or robbed some girls named Tiffany and Mercedes. I thought about it for a minute and came up with a solution. I'll just go the bank and deposit a little bit at a time, say $100 on each visit. But I quickly dismissed this idea, because I figured that somewhere along the line, maybe the twentieth straight day that I deposited a hundred ones, they would get suspicious.

So I did what any normal guy would do with $3600 in one-dollar bills. I went straight to the Uptown Cabaret. OK, I didn't do that. But I did consider it. Again. Instead, I did the next-best thing. I got another shoebox. I put it on the top shelf in my closet beside the first one.

A couple more years passed, and I kept socking away dollars in my sock drawer. (I'm cracking myself up. Socking them away in my sock drawer? Only a dad-joke master like me would laugh at that.) Eventually I filled my second money box. Then I started a third. As of today, I have close to ten thousand one-dollar bills in my money boxes. For the mathematically challenged, that's 10,000 dollar-dollar bills, y'all. That's right, ten grand is just sitting on a shelf in my closet. A closet that doesn't have a lock on it, in a house that doesn't have a security system. My money boxes have been undiscovered for close to twelve years.

Does it bother me to know that as soon as this story is published, people will know that I have a shitload of cash in my closet? Do I worry that now my house will be broken into and my stash of cash will be stolen? Not really. Odds are pretty good that I will get robbed. But if it happens, it should be really easy to find out who robbed me. It would be someone who read this book. Which would really narrow down the suspects to three people: my mom, my sister and you.

So don't even think about it!

Addendum

I have been advised by my editor, Betsy Thorpe, that it's not wise to have $10,000 in cash in my closet. She explained to me in no uncertain terms that it's just plain stupid to have $10,000 in cash in your closet and publish a story about it and tell everyone where it is. I've thought about it for a while, and finally realized that she was right. So I moved it to a different closet.

THE CHRISTMAS SPIRIT

Every year, right after Thanksgiving, I decorate the cedar tree in our front yard. I cover it with large old-school multicolored Christmas lights, the kind that were banned from indoor Christmas trees years ago because they were fire hazards. When I started doing this about twenty years ago, it only took three strands of lights to cover our cute little Christmas tree. Then it was only about seven feet tall. Now it's over thirty feet tall, and this year it took twenty-seven strands to cover it.

It's become an Oakley Christmas tradition and my personal obsession. Decorating it is a whole-weekend endeavor. And I totally love it. Because when it's done, we have our own Rockefeller Center tree right here on Crooked Oak Lane. When it's lit, it always puts me in the Christmas spirit.

Getting lights to the top of a thirty-foot-tall cedar tree is no easy task. But over the years, I've devised a jackleg system that actually works. I use two-inch PVC pipe, spray-paint each ten-foot-long section black, and attach the star and the lights to the end of the first pipe. Then I attach two more ten-foot pipes to the end of that pipe and push the star and the lights to the top of the tree.

Invariably, there are always a few things that I need to complete this project. And this year was no exception. I needed some extra PVC pipe, fuses, replacement lights, and some black spray paint. So, I hopped in the car and headed for Lowe's.

Some people would consider going to a big-box hardware store in the middle of decorating a Christmas tree to be a chore. But not me. It always brings back memories of going there with my dad, Sid. After I moved to Charlotte, each year on Christmas Eve, Sid and I would go to Lowe's to Christmas shop for each other. It was fantastic, because hardly anyone was ever there, so we had the whole store to ourselves. While everyone else was at the mall, we'd walk around and buy rakes, shovels, and drill sets for each other. Then we'd go home and wrap them and put them under the tree. A rake wrapped in Santa paper with a big red bow on it is a very funny sight.

When I got to Lowe's, I grabbed a shopping cart and smiled when I noticed a worn Scooby-Doo sticker on the cart handle. "Hey, Scooby!" I said to myself. I pushed the cart inside and started gathering my goods. I went to the Christmas section first to get replacement light bulbs. This is the part of the store where you'd normally find house-plants, but during the holidays, it's packed with every kind of deco-ration you can imagine. Even old-school replacement lights. I pushed my cart through the clutter and finally found them at the very back. I put twenty-four four-packs of lights in my cart. Six packs of red, six packs of green, and four packs each of blue, white, and orange. Even though I had about forty-eight extension cords at home, I grabbed a couple more—you can never have too many extension cords. Then I pushed my cart back into the main store. I went over to the paint aisle and found the duct tape and the black spray paint. I had no idea where to find fuses for Christmas lights, so I stopped one of the guys with the red vests.

"Where would I find fuses?" I asked.

"What do you need them for?"

"For Christmas tree lights," I said, holding up the tiny burned-out fuse that I'd brought with me.

"Automotive fuses are on aisle 6. But I'll bet they have packs of fuses for Christmas lights over in the holiday department. They'll probably be hanging near the back on little J-hooks like this," he said pointing to some tacks hanging on a shelf beside him. "If you don't find them there, come back and get some automotive fuses. They'll probably work, but they might be more expensive."

"Thanks, I appreciate it." I turned my cart around and headed back toward the holiday department. I still needed to get PVC pipe from the main store, but the pipe came in ten-foot sections, so I wanted to pick that up last. I went back into the Christmas department and pushed my cart through the crowded aisles looking for fuses. Maneuvering through the narrow spaces between the Norfolk Island pines and boxes of holiday accent rugs wasn't easy, so I parked my cart and walked toward the back of the department, where I had found the replacement lights earlier. I scoured each and every shelf looking for the J-hooks that the Lowe's guy had told me about, but I couldn't find them anywhere. *Oh well*, I thought, *I'll just go back and get some expensive automotive fuses.*

I walked back over to my cart. But when I got to where I'd left it, it wasn't there. *That's odd*, I thought, *maybe I left it on the next aisle over. Everything in here is so crowded it all looks alike to me.* I walked over to the next aisle and didn't see my cart there either. Maybe someone had pushed it out of the way. I walked over by the inflatable Santa playing golf with Rudolph and looked up and down that aisle—still no cart. I walked back to where I'd found the replacement lights and still nothing. *Did I leave the cart back in the main building?* I walked back to the entrance to the department and nothing. A weird sense of panic started to overtake me. Not because I had lost my cart, but because I thought I had lost my mind. I'd only left it there for two or three minutes. Had I developed a sudden case of what my mom calls CRS disease? Can't Remember Shit. Was I experiencing my first senior moment? I walked back where I thought I'd left the cart between the Norfolk Island pines and the accent rugs. But still no cart.

Then I saw it. Not my cart, but a package of red Christmas replacement lights sitting on a clear 4-inch saucer. It was on the top shelf of a "Grab a Seasonal Saucer" display of plastic holiday serving trays. On the second shelf was a pack of green lights and blue lights, and as I looked farther down, I saw the rest of my replacement lights. My mouth dropped wide open. Someone had dumped my stuff and pilfered my cart.

I looked around but I didn't see the black spray paint or the duct tape or extension cords. Maybe they were still in the cart. I looked around at the closest cart in sight. In it was a Christmas cactus and an orchid. Beside it stood an elderly woman holding another orchid.

"I can't find my cart," I said to her. "Did you see anyone push a cart out of here?"

"Yes, I did. I saw a lady get a cart a minute ago and push it out of here."

"Where?"

"In there," she said pointing back toward the main part of Lowe's.

"Thanks," I said, and I briskly walked back toward the main entrance looking in each cart along the way, hoping to see the black spray paint and duct tape still there and more importantly, confront the cart thief.

I looked in six or seven carts and saw nothing of mine, so I went back to the entrance to the store and got another cart. I couldn't understand why someone would go to the trouble of emptying my cart when they could get their own by walking seventy-five feet to the front of the store. I wheeled my new cart to the "Grab a Seasonal Saucer" display and started replacing the replacement lights into my new cart. As I bent down to grab the last pack of lights, I looked across the aisle, and right beside the Orchid Plus water-soluble orchid food, I saw my can of spray paint and the duct tape.

Well, I thought as I put them into my new cart, *at least I don't have to go all the way back to the paint section to get those.*

I pushed my new cart by the elderly lady I had just spoken to. I glanced at her cart with the orchid and the Christmas cactus in it, and I did a double take. I may have even done a triple take. On the handle of her cart was a worn Scooby-Doo sticker. I couldn't believe it. This innocent, sweet-looking little old lady had stolen my cart. Not only that, she had lied to my face about it and blamed it on somebody else. I looked over at her. She was still admiring the orchids.

"I can't believe someone stole my cart."

She slowly turned around to me, completely ignoring what I had just said and said, "Do you know anything about orchids? Are they hard to raise?"

I couldn't believe that this woman was asking me about orchids right after she dumped all my stuff and stole my cart. I wasn't really sure what to say. I wanted to confront her and say that her cart was actually my cart. It's got a Scooby-Doo sticker on it, after all. But she was so sweet and nice and innocent-looking.

"Orchids are very hard to raise," I said, "You have to be careful how much you water them, and you need to use the right fertilizer. I think Miracle-Gro is the right kind, but I'm not sure."

"Thank you," she said.

I stood there for a minute, just staring at the Scooby-Doo sticker. Then I looked at her and back at the cart. Just enough to let her know that I knew that she was the cartjacker.

I decided it was best that I finish my shopping. I pushed my new cart out of the Christmas department and went straight to get the PVC pipe. All the while, I kept asking myself, why was I such a wimp? Why didn't I confront the woman for stealing my cart?

I went back to the plumbing aisle and I took two ten-foot PVC pipes out of the rack and balanced them across my cart. I gingerly turned the cart around without knocking anything off the shelves and pointed it in the direction of the checkout aisle. Just as I got to the checkout, I realized that in the midst of all the confusion, I had forgotten to get the fuses. So, I turned the cart around and pushed it back toward the electrical aisle.

This time I wasn't as graceful in my turning. The end of the PVC pipe hit the corner of an eight-foot-tall display of pre-packaged Kobalt tool sets, and the whole stack crashed to the floor. As I stopped to pick them up, two thoughts went through my mind: One, I can't believe that lady stole my cart and two, if she hadn't stolen my cart, I wouldn't have been so flustered that I picked up the PVC pipe before the fuses. I would have gotten the pipe last and headed straight to the checkout, and I never would have knocked over this display.

The more I thought about the thief, the more pissed I got. Not only at her, but at myself for not confronting her about it.

I found the fuses, I checked out, and swiped my Visa card for $79.47. I carefully pushed my cart out the front door and through the parking lot to my car. I loaded my three bags into the front seat and rolled the back window down and slid the PVC pipe in the window. I grabbed my cart and pushed it back to the cart return.

As I let go of my cart, I knew I couldn't let go of the incident that had just occurred. I turned around, and instead of walking to my car, I started walking across the parking lot back toward Lowe's. I was going back in. I had to tell the lady that I knew she'd stolen my cart.

I walked toward the entrance to the garden department, and when I was about fifty yards away from the open-air checkout, I saw the cartjacker waiting in line to pay. Apparently, she saw me too, because she left her cart and walked two aisles over, turned her back to me, and started looking at the pansy display.

I walked up to her cart, which was third in line to check out, and inside it was a Christmas cactus and two orchids. My first thought was to remove the flowers and take my cart, but that would have been stooping to her level.

Instead, I had a better idea. I reached over and picked up a fifty-pound bag of Scott's Southern Gold Premium Fertilizer. Then I picked up another. And another. And another. I put all four bags in her cart. I looked over at her and her back was still to me in full-on avoidance.

I walked over to where she was standing and said, "By the way, I found my cart."

"You did?" she said with a look of surprise.

"Yes." I smiled. "And I just came over to remind you to get plenty of fertilizer for your orchids."

"Oh, thank you."

"You're welcome, and have a Merry Christmas," I said as I walked out of Lowe's and back into the Christmas spirit.

PART II

GROWING UP

After the 9/11 attacks in New York City, I had a lot of anxiety. Claire and I had two small kids at the time, and like pretty much everyone else in America, we were on edge. During that time, I had a lot of trouble sleeping. Part of it was due to the fact that I was binge-watching CNN's live reports from Ground Zero 24/7. I was simply overwhelmed with how horrific the events were. The city that I loved, where Claire and I met and started our lives together, was devastated. One night I decided not to watch CNN and I just went to bed around nine o'clock. I was exhausted and fell into a deep sleep. And I had a dream.

I was nine years old again and sitting with my mom in her pottery studio. She was sitting at her potter's wheel, kicking the wheel below with her foot to spin the wheel on the top. Her hands held a piece of clay that was turning. She looked over at me and said, "Before you make a pot, you have to get the clay centered on the wheel. It has to stay centered." The only sounds in the studio were the gentle squeak of the wheel going around and her voice. "If it's not on center, the pot will be a little catawampus when it's done."

It was serene, calming, and safe. It was so comforting to be there with my mom in her studio. When I woke up, every bit of my anxiety had gone away. I knew I was going to be fine and get through that period of time. To put it in pottery terms, the dream had centered me.

It may have been the best dream I've ever had. Because it made me realize that I had the perfect childhood. It wasn't your typical childhood. I was raised by two artists out in the middle of nowhere in North Carolina. Two hardworking people who started a pottery business and grew it into something that is iconic today, fifty years later.

My parents, Sid and Pat, at Cedar Creek Pottery, 1977.

I owe my parents a ton of gratitude for providing me with such an unusual and fantastic upbringing. Claire and I often joke around about how our kids won the parent lottery. The truth of the matter is, I won the parent lottery too.

Even though I ended up a little off-center.

THE VANGUARD OF PROGRESSIVE THINKING

My mom has always been on the vanguard of progressive thinking. I've learned a lot from her over the years. Even when I didn't want to.

My mom was the first person to ban smoking in her home in North Carolina. That may not sound like much today, but when she laid down the law in 1978, it was groundbreaking shit. Our house, which my mom designed without a degree in architecture, by the way, was built on the corner of a tobacco field. My father was a pack-a-day Camel smoker, who I'm sure was not too pleased with Mom's decree that he must smoke outside, but he abided by it. He had a little chair right outside our front door where he smoked for the next twenty-five years. As soon as I get the chance, I'm going to petition the governor to place a roadside marker at this historically significant site. The first non-smoking house on Tobacco Road.

My mom was the first woman to have her work on the cover of *Ceramics Monthly* magazine in 1972. Her innovative coil-built pinch pot design was seen by "envious craftsmen and women from coast to coast." None more envious than my dad, who *Ceramics Monthly* had come to interview for a feature story, yet somehow they put my mom's work on the cover instead. He was always a champion of my mom and her work, and was outwardly very excited about it. But even though his pottery and sculpture were featured prominently inside the magazine, page 37 and 38 are not the same as the cover. My dad might have been the king of Cedar Creek Pottery, but my mom was the ruler of *Ceramics Monthly*.

I think that's what drove him to perfect his zinc crystalline glaze that he used on his porcelain vases, which are now included in the permanent collection of the Smithsonian Institution. But enough about Sid.

This story is about Pat, my mom, who was also one of the first people in the South to recognize that gluten wasn't a muscle in your ass. Gluten was something that a lot of people had trouble digesting. Including her.

Which no doubt sucks, but we lost much of our empathy for her over the last forty-odd years of listening to her announce to anyone with ears that she was gluten free.

Whenever the Oakley family went out to dinner, Lisa and I always wagered on how many times she would say *gluten* or *gluten free*. The over/under number was usually seventy-five. And if you wanted to win the bet, you always took the over.

Did I mention that my mom is also in *Guinness World Records*? Since 1983, she has said "gluten free" 2,346,589 times. That's the record. Look it up. It's like Joe DiMaggio's fifty-six-game hitting streak. It'll never be broken.

But her amazingness doesn't stop there. My mom was on the forefront of the boxers-versus-briefs debate in the early 1990s.

Claire and I had been married about a year, and Mom was visiting us in New York for the weekend. Mom and I went shopping and somehow ended up in the men's underwear section of a crowded clothing boutique in Brooklyn Heights. I remember it well, because it was the last time I went clothes shopping with her.

"Do you wear boxers or briefs, David?"

I ignored her, because who wouldn't have ignored their mom if she had asked them this question?

"I sure hope you aren't wearing briefs," she said, continuing to tell me—and the seven other shoppers within earshot—why boxers were far superior to briefs.

"If you plan to be a father someday, you should never wear briefs because they hold your testicles high and tight against your crotch, and that will overheat your sperm. It will cook your sperm. Sauté your sperm. Sizzle your sperm, and then your sperm will die. Do you understand, David?"

I wanted to run out of the store into the path of a city bus, but I was blocked by a young woman with four large shopping bags on one aisle and by a crazy lady, aka my mom, on the other.

"The testicles were made to hang down," she said opening her hand and moving it up and down like she was holding a couple of plums. "It's nature's way of keeping your sperm cool, keeping your sperm healthy and most importantly, keeping your sperm alive. I want to be a grandmother someday. Wearing briefs will not help me to fulfill my dream. Do you understand me, David? Boxers for you, my son. Always boxers. I'm buying! Let your balls hang low and swing wide. Some day that will bring me a grandbaby." Her Southern accent echoed off the racks of designer underwear for the entire store to hear. It was one of the most embarrassing moments of my life.

But you know what? She was right. I started wearing boxers after her words of wisdom imprinted on my brain, and soon thereafter, Claire and I had Sydney. After Lucas was born, I started wearing briefs again, and we haven't had a kid since.

I learned a lot from my mom. But I still eat gluten.

THE CEMENT COURT

When I was eleven years old, I wanted a cement basketball court more than I wanted anything in the world. My cousins Ken and Brad had one. Their driveway was paved, and my Uncle Sam had put a basketball goal on one end of it. It was state of the art. Our driveway wasn't paved. Heck, our street wasn't even paved.

That summer, my dad was building an addition to his pottery studio. One sweltering July afternoon, I was helping him build wood forms to pour the foundation into. As we were leveling off the forms, I asked him, "What time is the cement truck coming?"

"In about an hour," he replied

"Well, do you think there will be any left over?"

"Any what?"

"Cement."

(Where I grew up, cement was pronounced *C-mint*, the accent on the first syllable. It sounded kinda like the way a normal person would pronounce *semen*, except it had a *t* on the end)

"Do you think there will be any left over?" I asked again.

"I doubt it. I ordered just enough to pour this foundation. Why do you ask?"

"I really want a cement basketball court."

"What's wrong with the basketball court you have now?"

"It's gravel, Daddy," I said. "When I dribble, sometimes the ball bounces funny off a piece of gravel and goes out of bounds."

"Out of bounds?" He chuckled.

"Yeah. It goes all the way down the hill into the woods. And then I have to run after it."

"Seems like all that running would help you get in good basketball shape."

"I can get in shape playing basketball. Not running in the woods. I want a cement basketball court."

"You're old enough for your wants not to hurt you." This is something that he used to say all the time when my sister Lisa or I wanted something. I still have no idea what it means.

"Come on, Daddy, please," I said. He just stood there, leaning on a shovel in his sweat-stained T-shirt and clay-stained jeans.

"First of all, David, I only ordered enough cement to fill the fifteen-by-twenty-foot slab we're pouring this afternoon. There won't be enough on the cement truck to cover your basketball court."

"Please, Daddy, it'll be awesome, even if we don't have enough to cover the entire court. Just having a partial paved court would be the best thing ever."

"We haven't built any forms to pour the cement into. And we don't have time to build any before the cement gets here. The answer is no. Now go get me a cup of coffee."

I ran down to our house and opened the jar of Nescafé. I scooped two heaping spoonfuls of instant coffee and put them into his favorite coffee mug. I ran the faucet until the water was piping hot and filled the mug. I stirred the mixture until it was just the way he liked it. How he drank that shit when it was 90 degrees outside, I'll never know. I brought him his coffee and made one last pitch: "I really want what's left over for my court."

"You heard me," my dad said. "I said no."

The cement truck showed up a little while later. Jerry Jerome was at the wheel—a good friend of my dad's. Mr. Jerome backed up to the form we had made. He flipped a lever on the side of the truck, and the cement started pouring down the chute into the form. He guided it around until the entire form was filled with cement. We then moved the two-by-six back and forth across the top of the form to smooth the cement out. Half an hour later, we were finished. We did a great job—it was as smooth as a polished hardwood floor.

When Mr. Jerome was hosing off his truck, I asked him if he had any cement left.

"Not much, probably about a yard and a half," he replied.

"Well, how much is that?"

"That won't cover very much at all."

"Is it enough to pave a basketball court?"

"Naw, son, I don't think so."

"Maybe there's enough to get it started? And then you can pour some more the next time you're out here," I reasoned.

My dad interrupted me. "David, Mr. Jerome doesn't have enough cement left. You heard him."

"But please, Daddy, I want a cement basketball court," I whined.

"No. Mr. Jerome doesn't have enough."

"C'mon, Daddy," I begged. "We can add to it the next time he's here. Please, please, please . . . I want a cement basketball court."

Sid stood there quietly for a moment and lit a filter-less Camel. He took a long drag off it, looked over at Mr. Jerome, and said, "Jerry, would you mind putting whatever you got left over yonder on the driveway in front of the basketball goal?"

"Yes!" I hollered, grinning ear to ear.

"You sure about that, Sid?" Mr. Jerome asked.

"You heard the boy. He wants a cement basketball court."

"Well, all right," Mr. Jerome replied with a bit of a bewildered look.

Mr. Jerome turned the truck around and backed it up. When he got to the court, he pulled the chute down, lifted the lever, and cement started flowing out on top of the gravel. I was so happy as it covered the court. Then abruptly, it stopped. By the time it ran out, a six-by-six-foot area was covered, about fifteen feet from the basket, right around the free-throw line.

"Wait, that's it?" I asked, my jaw open.

"Yep, that's all I've got today."

"Well," I said proudly, "It's better to have some of my court paved than none of it."

"Yeah I guess so," Mr. Jerome said, not looking convinced as he hopped back in the cement truck and drove away.

My dad looked at me standing there and said, "It's getting late. I'm gonna go in and get some more coffee. Come on in when you get it all smoothed out."

So, I grabbed my trowel and started smoothing it out as fast as I could, but I wasn't having much success. It was getting dark quickly, and it was still around 90 degrees. The cement was setting up faster than I could smooth it out. No matter how hard I tried, I couldn't get it to smooth out. After about half an hour of trying, I decided to call it a night. *Maybe*, I thought, *gravity will smooth it out a little on its own overnight.*

The next morning, I woke up early, ready to go shoot some hoops. I grabbed my basketball and dribbled down our gravel path to my new cement basketball court.

In the dappled morning light, I could clearly see that paving my basketball court had not been my brightest idea. The cement looked like a big dollop of chunky gray grits plopped right smack dab in the middle of my court. It was about as smooth as a week-old oatmeal cookie, and twice as hard.

I kicked the cement to see if it might move. Nope. It was there to stay. Permanent. I tried to dribble my basketball over it, but the ball bounced crazily off the uneven edges of the cement.

Well, this sucks, I thought. *How could I have been so stupid?* I'd ruined my basketball court. *I really should have listened to my dad. He was right.*

I guess he'd gotten tired of listening to me whine and decided to teach me a lesson. But I wasn't in the mood to acknowledge anything that he was trying to teach me. I resolved right then that I was never going to let him know he was right.

I decided to embrace my new cement court. I accepted it like it was and started playing more basketball than ever. I never complained about it. Never.

Even when my dad asked me about it. "So how do you like your new cement basketball court?"

"It's fine. I like it a lot." I never let on once that it was a royal pain in my ass.

"You know where the sledgehammer is, if you want to break it up and move that cement off the court," Sid said.

"No, I like it," I replied with a smile, thinking to myself that it would take two months for a guy my size to break up that chunk of cement.

I adapted to my "mistake" at the free-throw line. I learned to play around that area. I simply avoided the cement area of the court. I dribbled around it. I shot from behind the cement or drove to the basket and shot bank shots. I soon realized that having to deal with the gravel hazards that I hated actually made me a better dribbler when I played on a real court.

I became a decent basketball player. Not great, but good enough that I attended the Carolina Basketball Camp in Chapel Hill when I was fifteen. In one game at the camp, I made a move past the free-throw line, dribbled twice around a defender, banked it in, and was fouled. As I went to the free-throw line, I saw legendary coach Dean Smith standing behind the basket watching our game.

As the referee handed me the ball to shoot my free throw, Coach Smith nodded toward me, as if to say, *Nice play.* I dribbled the ball a couple of extra times, thinking *Holy shit, Dean Smith just saw me make a basket. And now he's watching me shoot a free throw with a chance to make a three-point play.*

I shot an air ball. It didn't even hit the net. Nothing but air. Dean Smith turned, said something to another coach, and walked away. It was one of the most embarrassing moments of my life.

It was all because that stupid cement was right on the free-throw line! I had never really practiced shooting free throws.

As soon as I got home from basketball camp, I got the sledge-hammer and started busting up the cement that was on my free-throw line.

And I finally learned my lesson: Always listen to your dad.

PERSONAL GROWTH

A cool thing about my dad, Sid, was his way of telling stories that were completely self-deprecating. One of my favorites he told at a party my parents threw when I was in high school. I can't remember the occasion, but the speech he made was classic Sid.

My parents had hired Robert Starling to be the entertainment for the evening. Robert had a local following in the late '70s in the Raleigh-Durham area, with his music playing on WQDR, the album-oriented FM station from Raleigh. I think my parents "discovered" him when he was playing at Manella's Italian Restaurant in Durham. Robert did a pretty good cover of Billy Joel's "Piano Man," and I recall that he had some originals that were decent, though I can't remember any of them. But that's beside the point.

Robert set up to play that evening in our house, which was designed by my artistic mom. Unlike most ranch-style home layouts of the 1970s, our home had high ceilings, exposed beams in the ceiling, and an open floorplan. Our dining room, kitchen, and den were all one big room. After a rousing, rowdy first set, Robert took a break. That's when Sid decided to step up to the mic of Robert's state-of-the-art sound system and begin his own performance. I had never seen my dad speak into a microphone before, and I never did again. I also had never seen him drink four rum and Cokes before, and I never did again, but what he said in front of the standing-room-only audience of forty people would not soon be forgotten.

"Let's have a round of applause for Robert Starling." He paused for some cheers from the partygoers. "I told y'all he was good. Thank you for playing tonight, Robert. And thank you all so much for coming to our party. It's really nice to know that me and my beautiful wife Pat have so many friends. And since we are among friends, I'd like to share with you all a story. A story of personal growth."

Everyone got quiet.

"Well, this afternoon, I took a nap," he said.

This came as no surprise to anyone who knew him. Sid took a nap every afternoon. I had never given much thought to what he wore when he napped. Which we were all about to learn, wasn't much of anything.

"I was having a peaceful nap until I felt something tickling me on my privates," he said.

"Was it Pat?" someone in the crowd yelled.

"I wish," he said. "I opened my eyes and looked down, and right on the end of my penis was a wasp. I jumped up out of bed, but when I moved the wasp stung me right on the tip. I yelled 'Motherfucker!' so loud Jack Hopkins probably heard me."

Jack was our closest neighbor, who lived a half a mile away.

"I hollered for Pat to come help. She came running and said, "Well, what do you want me to do?"

"'Suck the venom out,' I told her. She told me I was out of my mind and to take a cold shower." He paused for laughter.

"Then I jumped in the shower to see if that would cool the stinging, and by the time I got out, it had swollen up to about five times its normal size. The stinging stopped, but the swelling didn't. Five minutes later it was ten times the normal size. Which still wasn't that big, but it still was a lot bigger than it was before I took my nap."

The entire audience was enthralled. They were all doubled over laughing and looking at his crotch. Robert Starling was no longer the star of the show.

"The sting hurt like a bitch, but I guess it was worth it," he continued. "Because at least now I know what it's like to have a Johnny Wadd-size tool."

But he wasn't finished with his speech.

"I truly apologize for taking the microphone and telling such a long story, but I wanted everyone to know that from now on I'm not going to answer to Sid. I'm changing my name to Johnny Wasp."

I was on the floor laughing. I had no idea up until then how funny my dad was. I had no idea he was so good in front of an audience, and I definitely had no idea my dad knew who Johnny Wadd was.

But I soon found out where he watched his movies.

THE STARLITE DRIVE-IN

Yesterday was a beautiful December day in Charlotte. I decided to sit outside of the offices of BooneOakley to eat my lunch in the unseasonably pleasant 72-degree weather. I was joined by Steve Lasch and Mary Gross, two writers from our creative department. Somehow, we started talking about murals and how they were popping up everywhere in our city these days. Mary looked across our parking lot at the vacant wall of a new building that had just been built. The bottom two floors were plain, ugly concrete. "That would be a great place for a mural," Mary said. "Or maybe we could paint it white and show movies on it."

I hadn't thought of an outdoor movie in years.

"Good idea," I said, "We could have our own drive-in theater, right here in our parking lot." I turned to Mary. "Have you ever been to a drive-in?" I asked, wondering if she was too young to remember them.

"Yes, we had one in Lancaster, Pennsylvania, where I grew up. They would charge, like, $2 to get in, and we would sneak friends in in the trunk."

"What kind of movies did they show?" I asked.

"Not the latest releases. Movies that had been out for about a year or so."

"Did they ever show porn?"

"Porn movies?" she asked.

"I don't think they were called porn movies then. They were movies that were X-rated."

"Wait, they showed porn movies *outside*?"

"Yeah," I said. "You know what I'm talking about don't you, Steve?"

Steve, who is in his early sixties, thought about it for a second, and said, "Yeah, there was a drive-in theater near Boone, and they would show the X-rated movies starting at eleven p.m."

"Are you kidding me?" Mary asked, her eyes wide.

"They were real movies with plots back then," Steve explained. "But when you would get to the love scene, the actor and actress would go all the way."

"I'll never forget the name of the first one I saw," I said. "*Insatiable*. Starring Marilyn Chambers." I grinned. (I did some research and found that Marilyn Chambers wasn't the biggest star of Insatiable. That honor goes to Johnny Wadd Holmes. According to Wikipedia, Johnny Wadd was best known for his exceptionally large penis. I can attest to that. It was at least fifty feet long when projected onto the screen at the Starlite Drive-In.)

"I remember Marilyn Chambers," Steve said. "She was the Ivory Snow girl."

"The Ivory Snow girl? What does that mean?" Mary asked, crossing her arms and leaning back in her chair.

"Ivory Snow was a detergent. At the time it was probably as big as Tide. Marilyn Chambers's picture was on the front of the Ivory Snow detergent box. She was young and sweet and holding a baby. I suppose Ivory Snow was all about purity, cleanliness, and innocence," Steve said.

"Then Marilyn Chambers showed up as the star of an X-rated movie. Can you imagine how big that would have blown up if social media was around then?" I said.

"Oh, it was a pretty big scandal even so. Ivory Snow fired her and took all the boxes off the shelves nationwide," Steve said.

"It made Marilyn Chambers into a star. Well, that and the fact that she was hot," I said.

"So, who went to these movies?" Mary asked. "Did people just go alone, and you know . . . ?" Mary gave the international sign for jerk off.

"Oh no, you'd take your girlfriend . . . or your wife, I guess," Steve said. "You just wanted to watch for a while and then get in the back seat and have your own scene."

"Who did you go with, Oakley?" Mary asked.

"Sometimes, you'd just go with a bunch of guys," I said, "I know that sounds crazy, but that's when I saw *Insatiable*. I was driving my dad's van with my friends, Billy, Mark, and my cousin Ken. We bought a case of beer and were just riding around and drinking. Someone suggested that we should go to the Starlite Drive-In, and before you knew it, we were watching Marilyn Chambers.

I loved the Starlite Drive-In sign. Hard to believe Marilyn Chambers and John Holmes were fornicating on the other side.

"When the first sex scene was over," I continued, "the four of us got out of the car and walked across the parking lot to the concession stand. We got some popcorn and Junior Mints, and used the bathroom. We got back to the van in time to see the next sex scene. We ran out of beer soon after that, and decided it was time to leave. We drove out of the Starlight, being careful not to back over the tire shredders that were guarding the exits, to keep people from sneaking in."

"That is insane that they showed that kind of movies outside," Mary said.

"Crazy, right?" I said. "But what was even crazier was what happened the next day."

The next morning, I was working in my dad Sid's pottery studio, and he asked, "What did you do last night?"

"Nothing really," I said. "Me and some friends just drove around in your van for a while. We didn't go anywhere in particular."

"Did you go to Durham?"

"Yeah, we drove through Durham."

"Did you go to the movies?" he asked with a strange twinkle in his eye.

I wasn't sure where this line of questioning was going, but I was starting to get a little uncomfortable. I said, "No, we didn't make it to a movie."

"Well, that's really odd, because your mom and I went to the movies last night. We parked right behind a van that looked just like mine," he said. "That wasn't you?"

"No," I said and kind of laughed in a way that you do when you know you've been busted.

"It was downright uncanny how much the four guys who got out of the van looked like Mark, Billy, Ken, and you. They walked right by our car going to the concession stand."

I was in a state of total shock, disbelief, and disgust. *What is worse? Having your parents see you at an X-rated movie? Or knowing that your parents were at the very same movie?*

"Mom wanted to go over to your van and say hello, but I wouldn't let her because I didn't think she should embarrass you," he said.

"Embarrass *me*?" I said. "What about you and Mom? You two were at the Starlite, too."

"Yes, but we're married," he said, and laughed louder than I'd ever heard him laugh. "Now, let's get back to wedging this clay."

I looked up at Mary and Steve, whose mouths were wide open, and said, "Can you believe that shit?"

"That's gross." Mary said.

It struck me as funny that Mary used the word "gross." I mean, Gross is her last name. Anytime someone mentions something disgusting, people say, "That's gross." I'm glad that's not my last name. That's a big burden to carry through life. Almost as big as knowing your parents were at the same skin flick as you.

"Did you ever ask your mom about it?" Mary asked.

"No, I was way too embarrassed," I said.

"You should ask her about it now."

Maybe Mary was right, I thought as I was driving home from the office that afternoon. The great comedian Lenny Bruce once said, "Comedy equals tragedy plus time." It had been almost forty years since that night at the Starlite. Maybe now after all this time, it wouldn't be embarrassing to talk with my mom about it. It'd be funny.

So I decided to give her a call from my 4Runner. I wasn't sure that she would remember the incident. Or even acknowledge it. She answered the phone and was happy to hear from me. I didn't waste any time, unless you count the previous forty years. "Do you remember when the Starlite Drive-In used to show X-rated movies?"

"Do I remember?" She chuckled. "Of course I remember. What I remember the most was going to the Starlight with your daddy and seeing you and a bunch of your friends there. You drove Sid's van in and parked right in front of us."

"Oh my God," I said through my laughter.

"It was so funny seeing you there," she said.

"Were you embarrassed?" I asked.

"Not at all. I wanted to go up and knock on your window and say hi, but your daddy wouldn't let me."

"Thank God he stopped you. I never told any of those guys that you saw us there."

"Why not?"

"I didn't want them to know that my mom was watching an X-rated movie."

"David, just because you're a mom doesn't mean that you don't like to watch an X-rated movie now and again. It's perfectly normal."

Perfectly normal? Just like showing X-rated movies on a hundred-foot screen outside is perfectly normal.

Yep. I had a perfectly normal childhood.

PATIENTS

Sometimes I write a story and I'm so excited about it that I want to immediately share it with someone. Usually that someone is Claire. Sometimes it's one of my kids, Sydney or Lucas. Since this one is based on where I grew up, I decided to share it with my sister, Lisa.

I emailed it to her and ten minutes later, my phone rang. I grinned when I saw Lisa's name come up on my iPhone. I couldn't wait to talk with her about it.

"You're crazy. You can't publish this," Lisa blurted out.

"What do you mean?"

"You can't make fun of mental illness."

"Wait, what?"

"It's not politically correct. Mental illness is a serious issue in this country and it's not a laughing matter."

"But you just called *me* crazy."

"Yeah, I did. You're crazy if you publish this."

"Crazy is a slang term for people who have psychiatric issues. So, you're doing it too. You're making fun of crazy people by associating me with them."

"Whatever. I'm not printing it in a book."

"So, it's OK for you to call me crazy, but it's not OK for me to write about growing up in a small town where the main employer is a psychiatric institution?

"Yes, but you make fun of people with psychiatric issues."

"No, I don't. I make fun of our family."

"Same thing," Lisa said.

"OK, *that's* funny." I laughed. "I might put that in the story too."

"No, you're not, because you're not going to publish it."

Honestly, this was not the feedback I was looking for from Lisa. All I really wanted to do was make her laugh. But I started thinking about it and wondered if what I had written really was offensive. And it might be. But I've made the decision to include it in this book, with a precaution: The rest of this story is not politically correct. Mental health is not something to joke around about. For the record, I am not making fun of mental illness, I'm making fun of growing up . . . and my family. I will make fun of one person I am not related to (to the best of my knowledge) who sings while wearing only blue suede shoes. I apologize to him, even though he is almost certainly dead now, so it really doesn't matter.

I'm sure you've heard the phrase, "Don't lose your patience." I lived in Butner, North Carolina, until I was eight years old, and there it has a slightly different meaning.

Butner is the home to several state institutions. While the facilities' names have since changed to protect the innocent, in those days, they were known as the Murdoch Center for the Mentally Retarded, the Alcoholic Rehabilitation Center, CA Dillon Youth Correctional Center, the Federal Prison, and John Umstead Psychiatric Hospital.

They were always losing their patients.

From time to time, patients escaped. Or sometimes they just walked away when they were on lunch duty or something. Every few days, we would drive by a guy in work clothes walking along B Street toward Interstate 85. It didn't matter who it was, my Aunt Shirley would say it was a patient looking to hitchhike out of town. She said she could tell they were patients by how they were dressed. After hearing this for years, I just assumed if a guy was walking down the street and he was wearing a shirt and pants, he was a patient.

A few days ago, I was talking with my cousin Brad about it. He still lives in Butner. He told me that one time when he was about nine years old, he was riding his bike along 12th Street, and there was a patient standing beside the stop sign on the corner.

"How'd you know it was a patient?" I asked.

"He didn't have any clothes on," Brad laughed. "He was standing there with his hands behind his head swinging his hips from side to side like Elvis, singing 'Blue Suede Shoes.'"

"Was he wearing blue suede shoes?" I asked.

"I don't remember," he said, "But his junk was swingin' 'round and 'round in a circle. I ain't never forgot that."

When people ask me if I had a normal childhood, that was normal in Butner.

My Aunt Shirley worked at John Umstead. She was smart, and she used her "patients" to keep Brad, Ken, and me in line. If we were out it in the backyard playing basketball after dark, she knew exactly how to get us to come inside. She didn't have to threaten to give us a whoopin', which was a popular way to get kids to behave back then. She would just yell that Miss Cates down the street had just called and had seen two patients walking toward our house.

The thought of some Freddy Krueger guy walking down B Street would get us in the house faster than telling me that my Cheryl Tiegs poster had come to life and was waiting for me in my bedroom.

We had normal stuff in Butner too. Like youth basketball. But even that was a little off. We played at the Sports Arena, which was a really nice indoor facility, much too nice for a rural North Carolina town. It had fiberglass backboards and electronic scoreboards. It was nicer than the high school gym at the time. I didn't really think much about it growing up, but it turns out the Sports Arena was nice because it was part of the psychiatric hospital. And the guys who operated the scoreboards? Patients. Sometimes patients even refereed our games.

Can you imagine dribbling up the court and looking over and seeing the ref and recognizing him as the guy you'd seen singing "Blue Suede Shoes"? But hey, that was Butner.

In the mid 1970s, the State of North Carolina decided to build a zoo. They narrowed the possible locations for the state zoo to Butner and Asheboro. I had never heard of Asheboro before, and I was sure that Butner was the best choice. Finally, there would be a reason for people other than relatives of patients to visit Butner.

Not everyone shared my enthusiasm for the zoo to be located in Butner. My Grandma Jenny was one of those people. I was helping her tend her garden one summer morning, when she let me know exactly how she felt about the issue.

"I sure hope they put the zoo in Butner," I told her. "I think it will be awesome if they build it here!"

"You really want the zoo here?" she asked, a look of disappointment on her face like *How can you be related to me and be so stupid?*

"Yes." I nodded, but then started to feel unsure of myself.

"Not me," she said.

"Why not?"

"Because I don't want to be out hoeing my butter beans and look down the row and see a tiger staring at me."

"A tiger?" It was all I could do not to bust out laughing.

"Yeah, a tiger. Or a lion. I don't want no wild animal escaping from the zoo and surprising me in my garden."

"They'll keep the animals locked up," I said.

"That's what they say about the patients. Yesterday, one walked up on me in my garden and told me that he invented tomatoes. Then he told me that I needed to pay him for growing his invention."

"What'd you do?" I asked.

"I told him I needed to go get him some money," Grandma Jenny continued. "And I walked inside and called the Butner police."

"What happened?"

"The police came and got him and took him back to John Umstead."

"Oh."

"But if that patient was a tiger, he wouldn't have understood English and I wouldn't have been able to go in the house. Probably would've killed me right there in the tomato patch."

I started giggling like the fourteen-year-old that I was.

"Ya see, David, I can talk to a patient. I can't talk to a tiger."

"What if the tiger spoke English?" I asked.

Grandma Jenny narrowed her eyes and shook her garden hoe in my direction, and I took off running before I could find out what kind of crazy she was. Because by then I had figured out that in Butner, just about everybody was a little bit nuts.

Including me.

I'LL JUST CALL YA

When I was a teenager, I loved my Aunt Hallie's car. She had a 1968 Oldsmobile Cutlass. It was deep blue with a black hardtop roof. To me, it was a sweet-looking full-sized Hot Wheel. Hallie was proud of that car, and told me it had a four-barrel under the hood. I had no idea what a four-barrel was. I figured it must be something like a double-barrel shotgun, but twice as powerful. Whatever was inside that Cutlass, it sure went a lot faster than the four-speed Chevy Chevette our family owned.

I was talking with Aunt Hallie recently, and the conversation turned to that car. I asked her if she ever took it on any good road trips back in the day. "Oh, all the time," she said. "After me and Jay got divorced, me and Linda were always driving down to the beach." Linda was Hallie's best friend. "And let me tell you," she continued, "men noticed us when we were driving that car."

Hallie started laughing. "You're not going to believe this. One time, Linda and I were driving that '68 Cutlass back from a fun weekend in Myrtle Beach. We were cruising back up I-95 and we had just passed South of the Border. We were having a great time, cutting up and laughing about our shenanigans and all the golfers we met. The weather was so pleasant that we were driving with our windows down."

I thought, yeah, they were probably driving with their windows down because as nice as that Cutlass was, it didn't have air conditioning. Not many cars did then. But I didn't interrupt.

"I looked in the rearview mirror," Hallie said, "and noticed a man driving a gold late-model Lincoln following us." She didn't think too much about it, but twenty miles later he was still right behind them. She said to Linda, "I think that guy is following us."

Linda turned around to take a look and said, "He's not bad looking, Hallie." Then she threw up her hand and waved to him through the back window.

"Oh my gosh, Linda," Hallie said. "You can't be waving at someone on the highway!" Then she pressed her foot down on the accelerator and sped up to seventy-five to lose the guy. But the Lincoln kept up with them, and Linda kept on waving.

Hallie told me she looked back in her rearview mirror and saw the Lincoln change lanes. A few seconds later it was right beside them. The man looked over at them and waved and yelled, "Pull over at the next exit and I'll buy you a drink."

Instead of mashing the gas pedal through the floorboard to the front bumper and finding out what that four-barrel could actually do, she yelled over at him, "Where do you want to go?"

He yelled the one word that apparently must have been a complete panty dropper back in the mid '70s: "Hardee's."

"OK," Hallie yelled back. The guy in the Lincoln passed them and took the first Fayetteville exit. Hallie could've kept right on going on I-95 and lost him, but she put her right turn signal on and followed him up the exit ramp. At the first stoplight, the signal changed to red as the Lincoln was going through, and Hallie and Linda had to stop. They watched as the Lincoln headed up the road about a quarter mile and turned right into the Hardee's parking lot. Linda finally was the voice of reason and said, "We can do a U-turn right here and get out of here."

"Heck, we've come this far, let's go meet this fella," Hallie said, enjoying the adventure. When they turned into the Hardee's, the

Lincoln was already parked, and the man wasn't in the car. Hallie and Linda got out and went inside. They looked around and spotted him sitting in the back booth. "He was a nice-looking fella," Hallie said. "He was dressed in a sport coat and tie."

They waved and walked over to the table.

"You girls look like you've been at the beach," the man said with a thick eastern North Carolina accent.

"Well, you're right, we've been down at North Myrtle," Hallie said to him.

"That's a nice place," he said.

"Were you down at Myrtle too?" Hallie asked.

"No, I'm on my way back from a funeral in Georgia. A friend of mine passed away."

She told him she was sorry to hear that.

"Where are you ladies from?"

"I'm from Butner and Linda is from Durham," she said.

"I'm from Selma, a little town about fifty miles north of here," he said.

"Oh, I've heard of Selma," she said.

The guy then asked what they wanted to drink.

"Tea," they both said, "Sweet tea."

So he got up and went to the counter and got three teas. Hallie told me, "By the time he sat back down, we were all more at ease, and he really did seem like a nice fella. We had a lot in common. We were all from eastern North Carolina. He seemed to take a little bit more of a liking to me than to Linda. Maybe because I was a small-town girl and Linda was more of a city girl. She was from Durham. The conversation continued, and after we had been there for about a half an hour, the guy said to me, 'Selma isn't that far from Butner, can I call you sometime?'"

"Can you call me?"

"Yes, will you give me your phone number?"

"Well, I guess that will be all right." He took out an ink pen from his coat pocket and wrote the number on a Hardee's napkin.

"I can't believe I just gave you my phone number and I don't even know your name," Hallie said.

"I'll just call ya," he replied in his deep accent.

"No, you're not gonna just call me."

"Why not?"

"What's your name?"

"I'll just call ya."

Well, Hallie said she crossed her arms and started to get really annoyed with this guy. She didn't want some random guy calling her if she didn't even know his name.

"What's the problem?" he asked. "I told you my name."

"No, you didn't," Hallie insisted.

"I'll just call ya. My name is I'll just call ya."

"What in the hell are you talking about?" Hallie asked.

He took out another napkin and spelled his name on it. O-T-I-S C-O-L-L-I-E-R. Otis Collier. *Ah tus call ya.*

"Can you believe that was his name?" Hallie asked me. "Otis Collier!"

The two of us were cracking up. When I composed myself, I asked what I thought was an obvious question.

"Well, did Otis Collier ever call ya?"

Hallie's face turned from total laughter to a semi-frown.

"He did. And you know what?" She burst into laughter again. "That SOB was married."

THE FOUNTAIN OF SPEW

Remember stone-washed jeans? They were all the rage in North Carolina in 1984. That explains why I was wearing them in 1988 when my sister Lisa came to visit me in New York. I've always been a couple of years behind the fashion trends. Come to think of it, I was probably more than a couple of years behind. Because if they were in style in North Carolina in 1984, they were probably in style in New York in 1980, so wearing them in 1988 meant that I was nearly a decade out of style. But that didn't bother me. It really didn't matter what I was wearing. Because whenever Lisa and I get together, we have fun.

This weekend promised to be more fun than usual, since it was the first time we had seen each other since I'd moved to New York about six months earlier. I was the seasoned big-city guy now, so my plan was to take my little sister out and share some of the delights of the city.

I invited some of the people I had met at work and a couple of friends from college to meet us for dinner. We decided on Puglia, a restaurant in Little Italy known for its "authentic Italian cuisine" and atmosphere. What I later learned was that Puglia was really a tourist trap and about as authentically Italian as an Olive Garden. That didn't matter, though, because Lisa and I were together, we were drinking, and we weren't at a Pizza Hut.

Two fellow ad guys from Young & Rubicam, David Shih and Jeff Coleman, were there when we arrived, and had already snagged a table. Adam Kandell, a friend from college, and Guy Cosgrove, my roommate, showed up shortly thereafter. The waiter immediately brought over a bottle of red wine and six wine glasses. They weren't like any wine glasses that I had ever seen. They were stemless. They looked more like jelly glasses to me, but I guess if you poured wine in them, they became wine glasses. The wine they were serving wasn't in normal bottles that needed to be uncorked. That had already been done. The bottles didn't even have labels and looked like bottles you would see at a junk shop. The waiter explained that they made their own wine at Puglia and it was sold nowhere else. One taste told me he was lying. You could get this shit at the Mini Mart in Creedmoor. Under the label of Mad Dog 20/20.

After one glass, I asked the waiter to bring me a pitcher of Budweiser. Guy and I switched to beer, but the others, especially Lisa, took a liking to the vintage. Bottle after bottle and pitcher after pitcher were delivered to our table, interrupted only by six plates of chicken parmesan, which looked and tasted suspiciously like Chef Boyardee's finest.

A seventy-something crooner named Tony played an accordion and walked between the tables belting out "That's Amore" and other traditional Italian songs, like "Big Shot" by Billy Joel. The food wasn't particularly good, the wine wasn't great, and the singing was nothing to write home about. But somehow the combination worked. We were having a blast. In other words, we were so drunk that we thought the food was delicious and our singer was Tony Bennett.

When Lisa bet Guy that she could chug a carafe of red wine faster than he could chug a pitcher of Bud, and won the bet, I knew it was time to head home. The guys headed uptown for more partying, and Lisa and I hailed a cab. I soon realized that I didn't have any cash, so we decided to take the subway. It was only three stops and a lot cheaper than cab fare. Almost as cheap as the wine. As we waited for the 4 train, I realized how drunk Lisa was. She was telling me how cute she thought Guy was, but she wasn't really looking at me because her eyes were shut. Whenever she has too much to drink, Lisa talks with her eyes closed. She still does.

Finally, the train breezed into the station and we hopped aboard. There were maybe eleven people on the train, so we had our choice of seats. I led "Shut-Eye" Lisa to a nice seat near the front of the car, and we started rolling south.

Subway trains are without a doubt the best way to get around in New York. At rush hour, I could get from Grand Central to Brooklyn in twenty minutes. But this wasn't rush hour. It was eleven thirty on a Thursday evening. The train bounced along the tracks, stopping and starting and stopping again. We stopped in the tunnel under the East River for about fifteen minutes.

Lisa leaned forward in her seat and rested her head in her hand with her elbow on her knee. She quickly fell asleep. I put my left arm around her like the protective older brother I am. The train started again and lurched forward. We were bouncing and bumping all over the place. Lisa's head was moving up and down a like a bobble-head doll. Lisa's left hand was holding her head up. Her fingers were on the side of her head, her thumb under her chin and the palm of her hand was right under her mouth.

I didn't notice any of this before the fountain was turned on. What fountain, you ask? Not the fountain of youth, but the fountain of spew. Suddenly, red wine was being served again. Lisa's hand created the perfect funnel for the cabernet to flow directly into my lap. And flow it did. It was like a fire hose shooting out of her mouth onto my stylish stone-washed jeans. The puke that my jeans didn't soak up ran down to the floor, and when the train accelerated, it rolled quickly toward the other end of the car. Every time the train bounced, more wine would funnel onto me. Within seconds of the eruption, the other nine people in our car scurried to another train car. For the first and last time of my residence in New York, I had a whole subway car to myself.

When the train came to our stop, Borough Hall Station in Brooklyn, Lisa finally opened her eyes and looked me up and down.

"Damn, Dave," she said, "you're lookin' good."

"Lookin' good?" I asked. "You just threw up all over me."

"Yeah," she said, "but red jeans are in style this year."

Lisa didn't drink red wine for a long time after that night. And even though they were suddenly in style, I never wore those jeans again.

PART III

EMBELLISH AND EXAGGERATE

Recently, I was at a bar with my good friend Patrick Magner and a friend of his, a guy he'd gone to elementary school with. Patrick is one of the best storytellers I have ever met. He's always spinning tales about surfing in Nicaragua, driving at night with no headlights, or following the Grateful Dead.

He was regaling us with a tale of how, many years ago, he went on a first date to a Nirvana concert in a small club in DC. He got a drink at the bar with his date, but when the show started, he left her at the bar and joined the mosh pit for the duration of the performance—except for when he was lifted up by the crowd and thrown onstage while Kurt Cobain was singing "Smells Like Teen Spirit." He lost both his shoes and broke his toe, but when the show ended two hours later, Patrick limped back to the bar and his date was still there. "And a year later I married her," he said. "It was Margaret"—his wife of twenty-three years. Then he got up to go to the restroom.

As soon as he left, his friend shook his head and said, "That Patrick . . ."

"I know what you mean," I said. "That guy has some amazing stories."

"Well, I don't totally believe everything Pat says."

"You think he just made that story up?" I asked.

"No, I just think he really embellishes and exaggerates the truth."

I was kind of taken aback by this. I told Patrick's friend that all great storytellers embellish and exaggerate. That's what keeps your attention. It's a gift.

That being said, let me set the record straight about the stories in this book: they are not embellished. And they are not exaggerated. At all. They're completely made up. They're fiction. Total fabrication. There's not one ounce of truth in any of them.

OK, OK, I'm lying. There's no way in hell I could have just made all these stories up. I have a good imagination, but not that good.

You can't make this shit up.

FREEZE, CLOWNS

Not long after we were married, Claire received a curious letter at our apartment in New York. It was from the circus. The Clyde Beatty–Cole Brothers Circus in Winter Park, Florida.

She opened the envelope and read the letter to herself, then handed it to me. "What the hell is this?" she asked.

It was a personal letter from John Sheppard, the Director of Recruitment Services at the Clyde Beatty–Cole Brothers Circus.

It read:

Dear Ms. D'Andrea,

After seeing you in the Carvel Ice Cream commercial several times, we were surprised to learn that you are not a professional clown. Almost all of our clowning positions are filled by graduates of the Ringling Brothers Clown College here in Florida. However, once in a while we discover someone who possesses the rare, natural, and instinctive qualities of clowning that cannot be taught. We feel that there is a good chance that you are a "natural" in clowning.

We are interested in talking with you about the possibility of joining our company. I will be in New York City the second week in May for about ten days. I will call and hopefully we can set up an interview.

Sincerely,

John Sheppard

Director, Recruitment Services

ACME CIRCUS OPERATING CO., INC. PRESENTS

THE WORLD'S LARGEST CIRCUS

CLYDE BEATTY-COLE BROS. CIRCUS

BOX 1570 • WINTER PARK, FLORIDA 32789

April 16, 1992

Dear Ms. D'Andrea,

After seeing you in the Carvel Ice Cream commercial several times, we were surprised to learn that you are not a professional clown. Almost all of our clowning positions are filled by graduates of the Ringling Brothers Clown College here in Florida. However, once in a while we discover someone who possesses the rare, natural, and instinctive qualities of clowning that can not be taught. We feel that there is a good chance that you are a "natural" in clowning.

We are interested in talking with you about the possibility of joining our company. I will be in New York City the second week in May for about ten days. I will call and hopefully we can set up an interview.

Sincerely,

John Sheppard
Director, Recruitment Services

I couldn't help but laugh as I read it. "Sounds like you might be joining the circus," I said.

"Did you send this?" Claire asked, poking me.

"No! What do you mean?" I held my hands up innocently.

"I mean, is it real?"

"It looks real. And it's real funny." I started laughing again and fell onto the couch.

"The letterhead looks real. It's on real stationery," Claire said.

"There's no real way to know until he calls you," I reasoned, "and it says he'll call you in a couple of weeks. I guess we'll just wait and see if he calls you."

It's important to know this all happened pre-internet, so we couldn't have just jumped on LinkedIn and searched for John Sheppard at Clyde Beatty–Cole Brothers Circus. There was no way to verify it, so we tossed it on the dining room table with the Nobody Beats the Wiz circular and didn't think that much more about it.

At the time, Claire was the star of a Carvel Ice Cream TV commercial that was running constantly in the Greater New York area. In the commercial, Claire played the role of a clown.

Remember Tom Carvel? The gravelly-voiced owner and spokesman for Carvel Ice Cream? He would interrupt your Saturday morning cartoons to tell you how delicious his Cookie Puss cake was. Or invite you to send a Fudgie the Whale cake to your dad for Father's Day, because your dad is "A whale of a dad." Most people found these commercials a little weird and maybe a bit creepy. But boy, did Tom Carvel sell a lot of ice cream cakes.

Then the unthinkable happened. Tom died. So how does a company go on without their loveably creepy owner and spokesperson? They hire a snazzy New York ad agency to help them, of course. That's where I came in. While you may think of me as a suitably weird, creepy replacement for Tom, that's not what happened. What happened was Claire became Tom's replacement.

Not really.

But kinda.

I was working as a copywriter at TBWA Advertising, the agency that had just won the Carvel account. Copywriter is a fancy advertising term for writer. It derives from the early days of the ad business when most advertising was print. The copywriter wrote the headline and the copy in the ads that describe how wonderful a Steinway Piano is or how delicious Campbell's Soup is. When you say you are a copywriter, many people assume you are a paralegal or do something with copyright law. The most famous—if fictional—copywriter of all time is probably Peggy Olson from AMC's *Mad Men*. But back to Carvel.

My art-director partner and I were given the first assignment. We had to come up with a TV commercial to sell their newest product, Carvel Clown Cakes. It was simply a round ice cream cake with a clown face on it. To me it seemed like it would terrify kids, but we nevertheless started working on a television commercial immediately. We went through lots of bad ideas, and finally settled on one that wasn't as bad as the rest.

The idea we pitched was called "Clown Party." The commercial was set in a New York City apartment. Inside there was a party going on. But it wasn't a normal party. It was a clown party. Clowns would be doing clown stuff and making lots of noise. Just picture a normal cocktail party where everyone is drunk. Except at this party, the clowns are drunk. So, the clowns are making quite a racket. They are making so much noise that they disturb an old lady who is trying to sleep in the apartment below. We see the lady, in her bed, pick up the phone and call the police. We cut back upstairs to the clown party, and the clowns are out of control. They are juggling fire, swallowing swords, and doing all kinds of weird creepy clown stuff that I'm sure made Tom Carvel turn over in his grave. Then we cut to the police knocking on the clowns' door. The clowns don't hear the knocking, so the policeman kicks the door in. He pulls his gun on the clowns and yells, "Freeze, clowns!" The clowns all stop what they are doing and freeze in the postions that they are in. We then cut to a product shot of the Carvel Clown Cake, and the voiceover says, "Frozen Clown Ice Cream Cakes. Now available at Carvel."

Remember, I didn't say it was a great idea. But it was an idea that we sold to the new Carvel marketing team. Once we sold the idea, we had to figure out a way to produce it. Carvel had been used to spending about $3 on each commercial they made. They were seriously low budget. Not surprisingly, the budget we were given was not a lot more.

We hired Mitchell Walker to direct the spot, and he immediately said that he needed at least seven clowns for the party scene. We had the budget for five. So, we did a clown casting session and picked five fantastic clowns, three from the Big Apple Circus and two from the Ringling Brothers' Circus. These guys could do anything clown related. Eat fire, juggle bowling pins, and of course, scare the shit out of kids.

A few days before the shoot, the director told us that he really felt that we didn't have enough clowns to fill the room. It would look like a dead party, he said. We needed some extras. We needed some people to dress like clowns who could just be in the background. Our producer, Amy Shore, told the director we couldn't afford extras, but she said that maybe her husband Ivan would do it for free. It took me about one second to blurt out, "Claire will do it too." Mitchell was psyched.

That evening I went home, and during dinner I told Claire about our predicament. I told her we needed an extra clown and asked if she would consider doing it.

"When is the shoot?"

"Monday."

"I have to work on Monday," Claire said

"Take a day off. It'll be fun. Think about how cool it will be when our nieces and nephews see you in a Carvel commercial."

"What do I have to do?"

"Nothing, really. Just let the wardrobe people dress you like a clown, and you stand in the background of the clown party. That's it."

"That's it?"

"Yeah, you'll mostly just hang out with me on the shoot all day."

"OK, I'll ask if I can take Monday off," Claire said, and refilled her glass of cabernet.

I called Amy and let her know Claire was in. She said Ivan was too.

On Monday morning at six thirty, Claire and I arrived on set to shoot the commercial. We said hello to Amy and Ivan and the rest of the agency crew, and then Amy whisked Claire and Ivan away to makeup. About forty-five minutes later, Ivan walked in. He was dressed in a yellow clown costume with brown stars on it and a golden dunce hat. His facial makeup was done expertly: droopy eyes and an upside-down smile, otherwise known as a frown. He was a sad, mopey clown. His look was done well, but he didn't really look like a clown who was having a good time. He would definitely have to be in the background.

Claire was next. She was dressed like a cross between a traditional French mime and the Riddler from Batman. She wore a flowing white costume adorned with black polka dots. On her head was a beret, and her hair was down, framing her face. Her makeup was amazing: her face was ghost white, and her lips were ruby red. But the most striking thing was a black question mark that started on her forehead, circled around her right eye, and extended down her cheek to the dot, right next to the corner of her lips. She was striking. She had chosen wisely to take off from work, and I was psyched she was spending the day with me.

Now that we had the wardrobe done, it was time to begin filming the commercial. We shot the last scene first, the one where the clowns freeze and stand motionless. Mitchell was trying to compose the shot, which basically means he was trying to get all the clowns to stand in a place that would look good on camera. Claire was exactly where we expected her to be and where she wanted to be: In the very back of the shot, barely in view.

"There's something that's just not right about the shot. I just love the clown with the question mark on her face. And I also love that she's a girl clown. You don't see many girl clowns, ya know?" Mitchell said to the cameraman. "Hey you, clown with the question mark on your face. What's your name?"

"Claire."

"Could you come up here closer to camera, please?" Claire walked to the front of the room. Mitchell had her stand right in front of the camera so her face was filling at least a third of the frame of the shot. "Oh my God, that's perfect," Mitchell exclaimed. "Let's shoot this." So, we shot the first shot, with Claire right in front.

Claire Oakley, clown extraordinaire.

Everyone was happy with the first shot. Everyone except Claire. And perhaps the other clowns.

"I thought I was just going to be in the background," she said to me between takes. "I didn't agree to this."

"Oh, it's just for that one shot," I told her. "You'll be in the background the rest of the day."

"I'd better be. These clowns are scaring me, especially the one with the red nose and the big top hat. He's stalking me."

"What do you mean?

"I mean he's asking me all kinds of questions. He knows I'm not a real clown. He's making me really uncomfortable."

"What is he asking?"

"Where do I clown? Who am I with? Ringling, Big Apple, or some other troupe?"

"What did you say?"

"I told him I wasn't a clown. I told him I was an actress." At the time, Claire was working as an account executive at another ad agency.

"Did he stop asking you stuff then?"

"No, he asked what kind of actress! I didn't know what to say, so I said I was on Broadway."

"So?"

"Then he asked me what I was in. And I got nervous and I told him I was in *Annie*."

I busted out laughing. "You said you played Annie?" "Yeah, but it shut him up."

"Hey, Claire Clown," Mitchell called across the room. "Could you come over here?" He motioned her back on the set. "Here's what we're going to do in the next scene. I'll be filming in this direction and I need you to walk in front of the clown who's juggling the flaming bowling pins."

"In *front* of him?"

"Yeah, Claire Clown. We're gonna make you a star!"

Even though he was covered in clown makeup, I could tell that the juggling clown was not exactly happy that Claire Clown was cutting into his camera time.

Clowns take their shit seriously. What they do is extremely important to them. They don't clown around about clowning. And they certainly don't take kindly to fake Broadway actresses stealing their thunder.

But there was not a whole lot they could do about it on that day. Claire the extra became Claire the principal actress of the commercial.

And now the entire Tri-State area was seeing Claire star in the Carvel Clown commercial.

Now about that letter . . . A few weeks later the phone rang at our apartment. I answered, and a man with a deep voice with a slightly familiar twang of a southern accent spoke. "Hello, could I speak with Claire D'Andrea?"

"Could I ask who is calling?" I asked.

"This is John Sheppard with the Clyde Beatty–Cole Brothers Circus. Is Claire home?"

"Hold on a second, sir," I said and put the receiver down. Claire had just come from work and was changing clothes.

"Claire, it's for you. It's the guy from the circus!" I said, running into the bedroom.

"Are you shitting me?" Claire said, as she pulled a New York Giants sweatshirt on over her head.

"No, he's on the phone in the kitchen,."

"Oh my God, what do I say to him?"

"I don't know, just listen to what he has to say."

I followed Claire to the kitchen and watched as she picked up the phone. "Hello, this is Claire," she said.

"It's nice to talk with you too," she said.

"Yes sir," she said. "I was in the Carvel clown commercial."

"Yes, I was the clown with the question mark on my face."

I couldn't hear anything that John Sheppard was saying.

Until Claire turned red and demanded, "Is this Sid?" Then I heard the most uproarious laughter I have ever heard in my life coming from the receiver of the phone. He laughed for a good forty-five seconds straight.

Claire held the receiver away from her ear, looked at me and said, "Your dad is John Sheppard," and then she started laughing uncontrollably.

When they both finally got back under control, my dad explained that he had found the Clyde Beatty–Cole Brothers envelope and letterhead at the Buckhorn flea market, and devised the plan to solicit Claire to join the circus right there. He went home that afternoon and typed the letter.

"Well, why wasn't the letter postmarked in Creedmoor, NC?" Claire asked Sid.

"Because I know the postmaster, and I asked him to smudge it so you couldn't tell where it was mailed from."

Claire didn't have to join the circus. She had joined the Oakleys. And she would spend the rest of her life surrounded by clowns.

THIS IS GOOD?

I learned about Claire's family's obsession with presents soon after we were married. Claire is the youngest of four daughters, and her sisters, Pam, Mary Lou, and Chris were already married with kids when we tied the knot. So when I took Claire as my bride, not only did I get a wife, I got seven nieces and nephews, ranging in age from six to fifteen. Since I was closer in age and mental capacity to the nieces and nephews, I figured they would be easier to win over than the rest of the family. In most cases I was right. In most cases . . .

One weekend after we had been married for about six months, Claire and I left Manhattan to visit her parents in Rye, a picturesque little town about forty-five minutes north of the city. That weekend just happened to be Little Joe's birthday. Joe, Mary Lou's youngest, was turning six. Mary Lou told us that Joe was completely obsessed with the Teenage Mutant Ninja Turtles and was dying to have a Ninja Turtle board game for his birthday.

Before we left Manhattan, we stopped at FAO Schwarz, the largest toy store in the world. It's where Tom Hanks danced on the piano keys in the movie *Big*. This toy store was really big—three times the size of your local Toys"R"Us, with the prices to match. After walking around for an hour, we finally found the game he wanted, but the price was $39.95: twice what Claire and I had agreed to pay for niece and nephew gifts that year. But I remembered how obsessed I was with Batman when I was six, so I convinced Claire we should just go for it. It would be a gift little Joe would never forget. Plus, it was a chance to upgrade my standing in the family from new guy to favorite uncle.

When we arrived at Claire's parents' place, Mary Lou, her husband Johnny, and their kids were already there. We hugged everyone and exchanged pleasantries. Johnny asked if I'd like a cocktail. Just as I said yes, Joe bounded into the room. "Did you get me a present?" he asked.

"At least say hello, Joe," Mary Lou reminded Joe.

"Hello, Dave. Did you get me a present?"

"Well, happy birthday to you, big man. We did get you a present," I said.

"Is it a good one?" he grinned.

"Oh, it's a good one," I said.

"Can I open it now? Please?"

"Let's wait until after dinner, Joe, OK?" Mary Lou told him.

"OK, Mom," Joe said, showing amazing patience for a six-year-old. I guess he didn't realize that it was 3:17 in the afternoon. "After dinner" was still four hours away.

A half hour later Claire and I were in her room—well, the room that was hers before she was married to me. It was still her room then, too, but it was now my room, too, I guess, because I was now allowed to sleep in it. Anyway, we were unpacking our bags when we heard Joe.

"Dave? Claire?"

"We're up here." I called to him. He walked into the room with his cheeks flushed with excitement.

"What'd you get me?" Joe asked.

"We can't tell you."

"Why?"

"Then it wouldn't be a surprise."

"C'mon, what'd you get me?"

"Can't tell you, but it's good."

"Please, please, please," he begged, hands clasped together.

"We got you just what you wanted."

"You did?"

"Yep."

"What'd you get me?"

"Underwear," I said. I have no idea where this answer came from, but I looked at Claire and grinned.

"Underwear?" Joe said with a smirk. "You didn't get me underwear."

"Yeah we did, and now it's not a surprise."

"C'mon, what'd you get me?"

"I told you: underwear."

"Uncle Dave . . . ," he said, and as he left to go back downstairs, he gave me a look like he was enjoying this banter.

About an hour later, I walked into the kitchen, and Joe was sitting at the table helping his sister Melissa and his brother Christopher put a puzzle together. He looked up at me and said, "What'd you get me?"

"I already told you. Underwear."

He totally knew I was joking and said, "Is it something good?"

"It's *really* good," I said.

"Really?" he said excitedly.

"Yes, really good underwear." I walked back into the room to be with the grown-ups.

I was really having a good time with this back and forth with Joe. I had only officially been "in the family" for a few months, but Joe and I were really forming a bond. I was almost as excited to give him his present as he was to open it. Nothing solidifies the position of favorite uncle like the perfect birthday present. The way I saw it, the more I joked with him about underwear, the more appreciative he would be when he opened the Teenage Mutant Ninja Turtles game.

At dinner, Joe asked Claire again if we had gotten him a good present. "Oh, we got you a good present. A *really* good one," she said.

"A really good one?" he replied.

"Actually, it's a really good pair," I said.

"A pair?"

"Yeah, a really good pair of underwear." We all laughed our way through our pasta fagioli.

For dessert, Grandma Pam served homemade pecan pie, and as soon as she put it on the table, Joe asked again if we had gotten him something really good. I can't remember why we weren't having birthday cake. I think it was because Joe's birthday had been a couple of days before. Anyway, I looked at Mary Lou and said, "Well, it's after dinner . . . Shall we give Joe his present?"

"Why not?" she said, and poured me another glass of wine.

I looked over at Claire and she whispered to me, "We've got to wrap it." We excused ourselves from the table and said, "We'll be right back." We went into the kitchen and asked Grandma Pam for some wrapping paper. She said there was some in Claire's closet.

"Where'd you put the Mutant Turtle game?" I asked Claire.

"It's in a bag beside your duffel bag." I looked over and saw it. But something else caught my eye. My duffel bag was unzipped, and on top of my pile of clothes was a pair of my underwear. A sly smile crept across my face.

"Claire," I said, "let's really give Joe a pair of underwear." I reached down and grabbed the pair of Fruit of the Looms and held them up for her to see.

"Oh my God, that will be so freaking funny!" Claire said. "Hurry up, wrap 'em. He's been waiting all day."

"Hand me the wrapping paper." I quickly wrapped my size 34 tightie-whities into a neat package and put a red bow on top. I also wrapped the Teenage Mutant Ninja Turtle game in a separate box.

"Are they clean?" Claire asked.

"Are what clean?"

"Your underwear?"

I was a bit offended by this comment and answered indignantly, "Of course they're clean. Like I'm going to give a six-year-old dirty underwear for his birthday."

Claire and I hurried to the den where everyone was waiting, giggling the whole way. We stuck the "real" present behind the door before we walked in. Little Joe was pacing in front of the couch. Mary Lou and Grandma Pam were on the couch. Grandpa Joe was in his desk chair, and Melissa and Christopher were watching *Who's the Boss?*

"Turn off the TV. It's time for Joe to open his last present," Mary Lou said. Christopher clicked the remote. Joe was so geeked with anticipation he couldn't sit still. Just as I was about to hand the present to him, Claire broke into "Happy Birthday." Then we all clapped, and I handed the gift to him.

He tore into the paper like only a six-year-old can. As soon as he saw the white cotton material a look of sheer horror overtook him. All color left his sweet little face. He stood there holding his new pair of underwear for a couple of seconds with his mouth agape. He looked straight at me and uttered three words: "This . . . is good?"

Then he burst into tears. He looked around the room, found his mom, and ran over and jumped into her lap and buried his face in her chest. He was crying like I've never heard a kid cry. Completely sobbing. Like his whole life had been ruined.

Mary Lou looked at me like I was a complete moron. She was right.

Eleven-year-old Christopher looked at me and said, "Oh my God, Dave, how could you give that to a kid?"

This is bad, I thought. *I'm being reprimanded by a child. I've got to do something.*

I quickly went into damage-control mode. I ran to the door and got the real present. I handed it to Claire, and she said, "Here Joe, here's your real present. It's really good." He kept his head against Mary Lou's chest and pushed it away and through his sobs wailed "Nooooo!"

There was no consoling him. Sure, he eventually opened the game, but the damage had been done. I would forever be THAT uncle. The one who gave underwear to a six-year-old and scarred him for life. The thought of me ever being his favorite uncle vanished in a snap of an elastic waistband.

Thank God they were clean. There's no telling how he would have reacted if they'd been dirty.

THIS IS BETTER?

The Oakley family didn't invent the Christmas White Elephant gift exchange.

We perfected it.

The White Elephant game itself has been around forever, but we tweaked it in a way that can turn any boring family holiday get-together into forty-five minutes of not-so-horribleness.

The rules are simple, and anyone can play the Oakley way. We ask everyone to bring a wrapped gift not to exceed a certain price point, usually $20. Most everyone stays under the $20 limit, but sometimes we throw in a gift or two that's a lot over the limit. Like a bottle of Robert Foley wine, or a handle of Tito's vodka. It's in the spirit of the season. These good gifts are mixed in with the typical lame gifts that certain people bring, like an amaryllis bulb, or a pair of tube socks stuffed into a Milli Vanilli coffee mug.

To get started, we draw numbers from a hat to decide who picks their gift first. The person who draws number one gets the first pick of all the presents. It's kind of like having the top pick in the NFL draft, except that the person with the number-two pick has the option of picking the next present or stealing your selection. If they steal the number one pick, the first person selects another gift from under the tree. This keeps going until everyone unwraps a gift. At the end of the process, the person with the first pick gets the option of stealing someone else's pick or keeping theirs.

That's when most White Elephant games end. But not the Oakley version. Just when you think you're going home with an expensive bottle of wine, we add a twist to keep it going.

We bring out a pair of dice. Then everyone takes turns rolling the dice. If you roll a seven, eleven, or doubles, you *must* trade your gift with someone. Even if you don't want to. But before we start rolling dice, I set the alarm on my iPhone to go off at an undisclosed time anywhere between seven and twenty minutes. When the alarm sounds, the game ends. Whatever present you're holding when the alarm goes off is the one you win. Or the one you're stuck with, depending on your perspective. Mixing a religious holiday with a bit of gambling makes for a really fun time and a true Oakley Christmas tradition.

Even though it is the perfect game, there are those who think it still can be improved. Usually these are the people who win the lame gifts. And usually the people who win the lame gifts are the people who bring other lame gifts that they actually think are good. But I digress. Some people take this game way too seriously and get really pissed when they don't win the good gifts.

And when I say some people, I mean my niece Melissa.

"I always get stuck with the shitty gift," she complains every year. I always try to explain to Melissa that the game's not really about winning the best gift, it's about entertainment. It's about comradery. It's about spending quality time with your family.

"Well, I'm not doing this next year, because every year I get the stupid joke gift. I spend good money on the gift I bring."

"The Starbucks gift card?" I ask.

"Yes. I paid $20 for it. And I've got the receipt to prove it."

"Sorry you got stuck with the *I Party with Sluts* trucker hat I brought," I laughed. "Maybe you'll have better luck next year."

"I'm not playing next year." She crossed her arms over her chest and pouted.

"Well, if you think of a better way to do it, then let me know what it is."

"Oh, I'll think of something better than this idiotic game that gives me a fucked-up gift every year."

Melissa must have stewed on this for the next eleven months. On the following Thanksgiving at our house, just as we all were devouring Claire's famous pumpkin cheesecake, Melissa announced that we would be having Christmas Eve at her house this year. But more importantly, we would be doing a White Elephant gift exchange right after she served Christmas Eve dinner. But she had her own twist to the game.

"I have a way to make it fair and equitable for everyone who plays. Gift cards! All the gifts will be $20 gift cards!"

"Gift cards? That means everyone gets the same thing," I said.

"No, they won't. People will get cards from different places," she said, relaxing back into her chair, certain her idea was a winner.

"If we're going to do that, why don't we just all bring twenty-dollar bills and exchange them?" I asked.

"You just like the other way because you never get the shitty gifts. I figured you would have a problem with this idea, but if everyone gets a $20 gift card, everyone leaves happy."

"Maybe, but they'll probably fall asleep playing the game."

"No, they won't. Just buy a $20 gift card. Everyone likes a good gift card."

I looked across the table at Claire and rolled my eyes. "This is the dumbest thing I've ever heard."

"If you don't like it, don't participate," Claire reasoned. "It's as simple as that. What's the big deal, anyway? It's just a game."

"Yeah, it's just a game. The perfect game," I huffed.

After dinner I told Sydney and Lucas about Melissa's modification for the game. They hadn't heard our earlier conversation because they had to sit at the kids' table in the kitchen. It's one of the downsides of a small house.

The first thing Lucas said was, "Oh my God, why don't we just exchange twenty-dollar bills?"

"That's exactly what I said! It's so stupid."

"That's so dumb," Sydney said. "But I guess you could mix it up by bringing two tens . . . or four fives . . . or twenty ones." At last, validation from my genetic offspring. I guess we did raise them right.

"What about a five, a ten, and five ones?" Lucas said. We all laughed.

"We need to do something about this," I thought out loud, "but what?"

"I got it," Sydney said pointing her finger for emphasis. "We need to think of gift cards that we think are good, but Melissa thinks are bad."

"And only buy gift cards that Melissa will hate," Lucas said, finishing Syd's sentence.

It was a moment of divine inspiration.

"Like what?" I asked.

"Bass Pro Shop. She's probably never been in one," Syd said.

"Or the Uptown Cabaret," Lucas said.

"She's been in there," Syd said, and we all cackled.

At that moment, we dropped all our objections and decided to play Melissa's new game. The game designed to make everyone happy.

On Christmas Eve, we all gathered at Melissa's house. We had a wonderful dinner prepared by Melissa's mom, Mary Lou. After dinner, it was time to do the gift exchange. We put all the neatly wrapped gift cards on the table and Melissa explained the rules of the game.

"Basically, it's the same rules as the White Elephant exchange we do every year. You can trade three times, but we are not going to do the dice thing at the end this year. It takes too long. OK, everyone, reach into the hat and pick a number."

I got number one. Melissa miraculously got number 15, which meant that she got to pick last.

I selected a two-inch by three-inch card wrapped in metallic Santa paper. "I wonder what this could be?" I said as I opened my gift card. It was from Big Lots. I didn't even know what Big Lots was. Grandma was next and opened the first of four gift cards from the Oakley family. It was from Adam and Eve, the sex toy store.

"What the hell is this? I'm trading."

"You can't trade yet, Grandma; you just picked your gift. Someone may steal it from you," Melissa said. Curtis, Melissa's husband, had the next pick, and took the Adam and Eve card off Grandma's hands. Grandma picked again, and this time got a $20 gift card to Marshalls. She was thrilled.

The next few cards were from Costco, Stein Mart, and Off Broadway Shoes. Finally, it was time for Melissa to pick. She had the option of stealing anyone's already unwrapped card, or picking the last wrapped one on the table. She grabbed the tiny red gift bag with the gold bow. She eagerly unwrapped her gift card and her joyous anticipation quickly turned to outrage as she opened it.

"Burger King? Who brought this?"

"I did," Sydney said raising her hand.

"This is not what I wanted!" Melissa said, sounding a lot like Al Pacino in *Godfather 3*.

"Relax, you'll have a chance to get a different gift card when we do the dice part," I said.

"We're not doing the dice part this year, remember?"

"Oh, I forgot."

Melissa was right about her new version of the exchange: It turned out to be the perfect game. The only thing that could have made it better was having our nephew Joe there. I really think he would have loved the Fruit of the Loom gift card I brought.

DRIVES 'EM CRAZY

When our kids were growing up, we spent a lot of vacation time at Claire's parents' home in Vero Beach, Florida. It was fun for a few days, but usually around day four, Sydney and Lucas would be bored out of their minds. How did I know this? Because they suggested that we do something even more boring than sitting around their grandparents' house: They wanted to go fishing.

Now, I have nothing against fishing. I've done it many times. But for fishing to be enjoyable, I find it helps to mix in a few beers, and maybe even a joint. That way you can stare at a little bobber floating without a bite for hours, and you can still have the time of your life. Lucas and Sydney would not be fishing with the help of Budweiser and ganja, at least not that I know of at the tender ages of eleven and fourteen, so I wasn't holding out a lot of hope that this would be the highlight of their trip.

We borrowed three rods and reels from Grandpa Joe and Grandma Pam's neighbors—well, we didn't technically "borrow" them. We just took them. They were out of town and were nice enough to let us park our car in their garage. It's hot in Florida, so a garage is a big help. It cuts down on the "Ow, ow, ow, the seats are burning my legs!" howls from the kids. Which when we got the use of the garage, became promptly replaced by, "The car's all the way across the street. Can you go get it and pick us up?" I liked having access to their garage. The way I saw it, whatever was in said garage was mine that week. Their fishing poles, their tackle box, their case of Budweiser. Plus a little treasure that I found on top of their refrigerator: their "Pistol-Packing Hotties" issue of *Guns and Ammo* magazine with a woman holding a rifle wearing what I assumed was a camo bathing suit on the cover.

We had everything that we needed to go fishing, except for bait. Grandpa Joe told us there was a bait shop about four miles away in the little town of Wabasso. He offered to go with us, but there still were still six holes to play in the Hartford Open golf tournament on TV, and he didn't want to miss any of the scintillating rapid-fire action, so we ventured out without him.

I walked over to the neighbor's garage and got our car. I drove back and picked Lucas up. The two of us left the gated Island Club, where Grandma Pam and Grandpa Joe lived, to venture back out into the real world. I was psyched to go to a bait shop. Which probably was a good indication that Sydney and Lucas weren't the only ones who were bored. We crossed the Indian River Bridge, and in a couple of minutes we were parking in front of Wabasso Express Hunting and Fishing. It was 5:25 p.m. and they closed at 5:30. The front door was still open, but the steel bars were slid halfway across the opening. Lucas, who was eleven at the time, and I ventured in. I didn't see anyone in the shop, so I half-shouted, "You guys still open?"

A deep female voice replied from behind a shelf in the back of the store, "Yes, we're about to close, but you boys come on in."

The store smelled like, well, a bait shop. The scent of old fish, dead crickets, and bloodworm excrement filled our nostrils. It certainly smelled like a place where you could get the right bait to catch a fish.

Or a man; I was about to learn.

The woman who was running the place walked around the last aisle. She was heavyset, and looked to be in her late thirties, with bleached-blond hair, ruby-red lipstick, and a tight-fitting T-shirt that said, *Fishermen have bigger poles.*

She looked me up and down like she was sizing me up for dinner.

Her eyes widened, and a lazy smile came over her face. She said, "Hi there, my name's Tammy. What can I get for you boys?"

"My son Lucas and I are going fishing in the river. What kind of bait do we need to catch some fish?"

She looked at Lucas and said, "How old are you, son?"

"Eleven," Lucas replied.

"Are you a fisherman?"

He nodded and stood up straighter. "I've been fishing before."

"You ever fished in this river?"

"No," Lucas said.

"That's what I thought," she said back to him. "It's different in the river."

"Why?"

"In the river, you need something stinky to get the fish's attention. Real stinky. You need some real stinky shrimp. Come with me."

She walked over to a freezer and reached inside. "I keep this frozen, cause it's real stinky," she said as she handed a ziplock bag of shrimp to Lucas.

He smiled and held the bag at arm's length and said, "Phew. It does stink."

"But the fish love it," she said. "It drives 'em crazy."

I smiled and asked where the bobbers were. She said they were on the wall in the back. Then I asked her about fishhooks, and she showed us where they were. Lucas and I went back to the counter with our bobbers and our hooks, and Tammy said, "Can I get you boys anything else?"

"I guess that'll do it, unless you think we should get some of those, Lucas." I said, pointing to a display rack beside us. In bold letters it said, *Wilderness Dreams*. Hanging below was an assortment of camouflage bras, panties, tube tops, nighties, and thongs.

I pointed to the camo thongs and said to Lucas, "You think your mom would like a pair of these?" He smiled and rolled his eyes, no doubt a bit embarrassed about thinking of his mom camouflaging her private parts.

"I'm wearing a pair of them camo thongs right now," Tammy said. "They feel really nice."

I must admit that I got a little embarrassed thinking of this woman wearing a thong. The only thing I could think of to say was, "Ahhh, are they good quality?"

"Yeah, nicer than the Victoria Secret stuff I normally wear," she said. "They wash real easy too."

One minute ago, I was making a joke to Lucas about camouflage underwear. Now I really felt like I would be insulting Tammy if I didn't buy a pair.

"What size do you think your mom wears?" I said to Lucas.

He gave me a look that said *How in the hell am I supposed to know what size thong my mom wears and I really don't want to know.*

"Well, how much does she weigh?" Tammy asked.

I looked at Tammy and knew that she was twice the woman Claire was. Literally. So, I said, "One twenty-five, maybe one thirty."

"How tall is she?"

Shit, I thought, I didn't want her to think that I was married to some skinny bitch, which is what I'm sure she would have called Claire if she saw her.

"Five foot eight . . . I mean, five foot even," I said.

"OK, you should get her a medium," she said. I was relieved she didn't say small.

"I'll get her a medium. What do you think, Lucas?" He rolled his eyes at me again.

Tammy added up our purchases. "One pack of hooks. Three bobbers. One bag of stinky shrimp. And one camo thong. That'll be $14.67."

I paid her cash, and when she was making change, I asked a question that I really wished I hadn't asked, "Who usually buys these?"

"You mean the underwear?

"Yeah."

"Usually women," she said. "Women whose husbands are hunters. When those men come home from spending all day deer hunting and see their woman wearing nothing but a little camo, they can't resist it." She looked at Lucas and then at me. "Your daddy knows what I'm talking about."

I just grinned a little.

"It's the same way a fish reacts to that stinky shrimp. It drives 'em crazy."

I thanked her for her help, and Lucas and I walked out the door. Tammy came to lock the door behind us and said, "You boys bring me some pictures of what you catch."

We climbed into the car, I turned and looked at Lucas in the back seat.

"I know what I would have caught if I stayed there, Lucas," I said. "Gonorrhea!"

"What kind of fish is that?" Lucas asked, scrunching up his face.

"One that you wouldn't want to eat," I said and put the car into reverse.

We drove back to the house and picked up Sydney. The three of us spent the afternoon fishing off the dock in the Indian River behind Pam and Joe's place. Tammy was right: that stinky shrimp worked. We caught a lot of fish. Trout, redfish, and river bass. We let them all go, so all we had to take home to prove our success was pictures. Pictures for Tammy, and a special present for Mom.

Did the camo thong become Claire's favorite underwear? I can't say for sure, but at least she didn't burst into tears when I gave it to her.

JUST NUKE IT.

According to the US Bureau of Labor Statistics, 95 percent of US households own a microwave. Which means, according to the David Oakley Bureau of Statistics, that 5 percent don't own a microwave. This is not by choice. It's because they are poor and can't afford one. That's the only possible reason that you wouldn't own a microwave.

Unless you are the Oakleys.

We don't have a microwave in our home. Why? Because in 1990, Claire decreed that our home would forever be microwaveless.

"It's bad energy, she said. "There's no way that eating food that's been nuked can be good for you." I went along with it at the time, figuring that it was just a phase she was going through.

But almost thirty years have passed, and we still don't have one in our house.

I didn't have one growing up, so it really wasn't that big a deal. I got used to not having one. That being said, every once in a while, it would be nice just to nuke a bowl of soup, a slice of leftover pizza, or a Hot Pocket for dinner.

But when our kids were babies, I really wanted one. Have you ever had to warm up a bottle of milk for a baby without one?

For those of you who have microwaves, which would be everyone, I will explain how this works: You hear your child crying in the middle of the night. You groggily open one eye and see the blue digital numbers on clock that read 3:56. You hope the crying will stop, but

DAVID OAKLEY

you know that it won't, so you drag yourself out of the warm bed and stumble into the kitchen.

You reach into the cabinet and get a pot and fill it with about three inches of water. You place it on the stove and turn it on high. Then you open the fridge and just stare blankly inside for about five minutes while you're waiting for the water to boil.

When the water starts to boil, you open the freezer and get out one of the bottles of breast milk your wife has left. You take it out and place it in the boiling pot of water, taking care not to burn the shit out of your hand.

Did I mention that you are still half asleep? Or half drunk?

Now you wait for the boiling water in the pot to warm the frozen-solid breast milk to a nice temperature. If it's too cold, the baby will not drink it. If it's too hot, it will burn the baby's mouth.

There's not a specific time that it takes for the breast milk to get to the right temperature. But normally it takes between seven minutes and . . . ? Forever? How do you know it's the right temperature? It would be really nice if the bottle had a thermometer on it. (Note to self: I should invent that.)

The only way to know if the milk is the right temperature is to test it on yourself. Which means you use metal tongs and lift the bottle from the boiling water and put it on the counter. Then you grab a towel and pick the bottle up. Then you press the nipple on top of the bottle to squirt some milk out on your wrist.

If it scalds your wrist, it's too hot. If it feels like you just spilled Budweiser on your arm, then it's too cold. If it feels the same as when your kid peed on you when you were changing his diaper earlier that night, it's perfect. Did I mention that you have to do all this with one hand? That's because your other hand and arm are holding a crying, hungry baby. When you finally get the temperature right, you give the bottle to your baby and you go back to bed. Elapsed time, thirty to forty-five minutes.

I went through this same routine most every night when Lucas and Sydney were babies. Honestly, I thought nothing of it. It was just what you did as a parent. But I was wrong. It's what you do if you don't own a microwave.

I had no idea how bad I had it. Until our friend Marsha informed me about how it was in her world. "Oh, I just grab two bottles, stick 'em in the microwave for fifteen seconds, and then I pop 'em right in Mac and Madison's mouths. I'm back asleep in three minutes. Nothing to it." Marsha had twins and was getting it done in a tenth of the time.

Later that evening, I mentioned to Claire that I was thinking of getting a microwave.

"For what?"

"To save time in the middle of the night. Marsha told me that she warmed up Mac and Madison's bottles in the microwave. And it only takes, like, fifteen seconds."

"We're *not* going to warm up my kids' bottles in a microwave."

"But we'll get more sleep."

"How could you sleep after using radioactive waves to warm up my breast milk?"

I guess she had a point. So, we continued LWM: Life Without Microwave.

About ten years later, Lucas and I were watching TV one afternoon and the doorbell rang. It was Alan, a kid from the neighborhood, dressed in his Boy Scout uniform. I opened the door.

"Hi, Mr. Oakley. Here's the popcorn that you ordered from me last month. Thanks for supporting scouting."

"Thanks Alan," I said as he walked away. I looked at the box of popcorn, and I called to him, "Wait a minute, Alan. This isn't what I ordered."

He turned around and took out his order sheet and said, "It says here, Mr. Oakley, you ordered one box of popcorn."

"Yeah, but this microwave popcorn."

"It's the only kind we sell now, sir."

I walked back inside and said to Lucas, "Put your coat on. We're going to Lowe's."

"What for?"

"We're going to buy a microwave."

"But Mom doesn't allow microwaves in the house."

"I know that. Do you want some popcorn?"

"Yes."

"OK, then. Let's go."

Twenty minutes later, we were the proud owners of the cheapest microwave Lowe's sold: a $39.95 Amana. It certainly wasn't top of the line, but it had a popcorn button on it. And that's all we needed.

As I drove the car into the garage, Lucas asked me, "Where are we going to put it?"

"We'll find a place. How about right there?" I said and pointed to a space on a shelf beside my toolbox.

"The garage!" Lucas laughed. "It won't be in the house."

"That's right." I grinned.

And it's been there ever since.

P. S. Hard to believe that it's been ten years since Lucas and I installed our secret popcorn maker. I guess you're wondering what Claire thinks of our microwave. I'll let you know as soon as she notices it.

NOBODY EATS PARSLEY

These days, profanity in songs is so commonplace that we hardly even notice it anymore. But it wasn't always that way.

The first song that I ever heard a cuss word in was "Bad, Bad Leroy Brown." *Did that guy just sing "damn"?* I wondered at ten years old as my mom drove our Chevy Vega down Highway 50 on the way to the Crabtree Valley Mall. I listened and heard the chorus again—sure enough, Jim Croce belted out that Leroy Brown was the "baddest man in the whole *damn* town." I couldn't believe it. I couldn't believe that someone would actually record a song with a cuss word in it, and I really couldn't believe that WKIX in Raleigh hadn't censored it.

Instantly, it became my favorite song.

Several years later, the Eagles turned it up a notch. In "Life in the Fast Lane," Don Henley sang, "we've been up and down this highway, haven't seen a goddamn thing." I mean, this wasn't a *damn*, it was a *goddamn*. And they played it on WQDR-FM. It was almost scandalous. But once again, I had a new favorite song. As a teenager, being able to sing along to *goddamn* in the Bible Belt was pretty damn cool. Actually, it was pretty *goddamn* cool.

So, it's pretty well established that damn is a cuss word. And of course, if damn is a cuss word, then goddamn is most certainly a cuss word. Which begs a bigger question: What is the ultimate cuss word? My vote would be for pussy. It's not really a cuss word, but it sure gets treated like one.

I believe that Tom Jones was the first recording artist to sing about pussy. Or pussycats. When Tom sang, "What's new, pussycat?" I honestly believed he was just singing to his cat. He might have had a Tabby, a Siamese, or a Maine Coon cat. I didn't know. But he probably just got out of bed one morning, saw his cat and said hey, "What's new, kitty cat?" Maybe he thought that *kitty* cat didn't sound that good in a song, so he changed it to *pussycat*. And it became a huge hit.

I'd like to show you the lyrics to Tom's song "What's New Pussycat" here, but I'm not allowed to reprint song lyrics without the permission of the artist. I'm not even sure Tom Jones is still alive, but I'm erring on the side of caution here. I don't want to get sued, or even worse, get my ass kicked by an eighty-year-old sex symbol from the 1970s.

OK, even though I can't reprint Tom's lyrics, I can talk about them. A delicious pussycat? I mean, Tom, who eats a pussycat? Then he goes on to sing about kissing your sweet little pussycat lips. C'mon. Who actually kisses a cat on the lips? No one, unless they want to get the shit scratched out of them. And more importantly, does a pussycat even have lips?

I truly thought the song was about cats until I imagined the lyrics if you dropped the *cat* part. It certainly changes the connotation of the song. Check out the lyrics for yourself online. I'll just wait here. . . .

See what I mean?

It's like an old joke my Uncle Pete used to tell: "What's the difference between parsley and pussycats? Nobody eats parsley."

Same thing with the joke: It's much better without the *cats*.

Maybe that's how Tom Jones got around the censors. He added *cat* and the song became cute, but the whole time he was singing about cunnilingus. No wonder it was such a big hit.

Since then, I've always thought that if someone came out and sang a song just about pussy, you'd have a huge international hit. It would go straight to number one—and Cardi B and Megan Thee Stallion have recently proved me right. But for many years, I figured folks were way too uptight for that . . . until I happened to be in a surf shop in Miami in 2002.

Claire and I were in South Beach with our friends Tom and Susan Watts and Chris and Cindy Maese to see the Carolina Panthers play the Miami Dolphins. The day before the game, we were shopping for beach towels when a song came on the surf shop's sound system that immediately caught my ear. The beat was infectious. The lyrics were kinda suggestive, but certain words were censored. I knew that I had to find out who sang it, and more importantly, what words they were bleeping out.

Since this was pre-smartphone, I asked the girl behind the counter if she knew the song and she said she had no idea. But she suggested that I might be able to find it at a hip-hop music shop a few blocks away. Chris and I told the rest of the group we had an errand to run and that we'd meet them back at the hotel. Ten minutes later we were in a record store.

"We heard a song a little while ago . . . we don't know who sings it, but it went something like this . . . 'My neck, my back, lick my beep and my beep.'"

"Oh yeah, that's Khia. Her new CD is right over there." The store manager pointed to the new releases.

On the top of the new releases rack was a CD that had a woman on the cover on her hands and knees looking up toward me. In big bold type it said *KHIA: THUG MISSES, featuring "My Neck, My Back."* I thought this was it, but when I saw the *PARENTAL ADVISORY: EXPLICIT LYRICS*, I knew for sure that we'd found what we were looking for. We bought it and headed back to meet the rest of the crew at our hotel in South Beach.

Claire and I invited everyone to come over to our room for a cocktail before we went out for dinner that night. When they arrived, we had Khia playing full blast. Without a doubt it was one of the catchiest songs I'd ever heard. And throughout its unedited, uncensored brilliance was the ultimate cuss word: *pussy*.

I'd like to print the lyrics here, but I don't have permission, and I know that Khia is still alive, and I definitely know that she would kick my ass if I used them without permission. So again, I have erred on the side of caution.

If for some strange reason, you have never heard this song, please put this book down and listen to it on Spotify or iTunes immediately.

We all listened in disbelief at this amazing ditty. It was like nothing we had ever heard. It was dirty. It was graphic. But best of all, it was extremely funny. For the rest of the weekend, we couldn't get it out of our heads.

It was such a wonderful song that you didn't even need to say the *pussy* part to get your point across. All you had to do was say, "My neck, my back," and it would cause reactions ranging from grins to giggling to straight up gut-punch laughing. It is, in my humble opinion, a straight up work of genius. A masterpiece.

When we got back to Charlotte, I couldn't wait to introduce the song to our family and friends. I got my opportunity on Cinco de Mayo, 2002. That's May 5 for those of you who don't speak Margarita.

Not only was May 5 the anniversary of a great Mexican Army triumph, it was also a big day for the Oakley family. Every family member from New York to Florida made the trip to Charlotte that day for a very special event.

They all came to town to witness our daughter Sydney, and a hundred other little girls and boys dressed like mini-brides and mini-grooms, walk down the aisle and take a bite of a tasteless round wafer, forever cementing their allegiance to the Catholic Church. A spectacle otherwise known as first Holy Communion. And what better day than a holy day to introduce our family to a song about a very holy place.

The spring ritual was over in an hour and a half, even though it seemed like five hours. Immediately after, we all gathered in the fellowship hall to shake hands and have our pictures taken with the priest and the kids. We were all on our best "participating Catholic" behavior.

At the fellowship hall, G.W. and Mary Mix invited the adults in our family to come over to their house that evening for a Cinco de Mayo party. G.W. and Mary always threw great parties, and G.W. was promising to make pitcher after pitcher of his famous top-shelf margaritas to celebrate. We left the reception, changed our dresses and suits for T-shirts and flip-flops, fed the kids, and left them with Janet, our babysitter. Now we were ready to start the real celebration.

Claire's sister Pam and her husband, Rob, and their daughter, Lindsay, got in our car, and we headed over to the Mix residence. My sister, Lisa, and her husband, Craig, followed in their car. G.W. met us at the door with a pitcher of margaritas and poured each of us a giant glass full of that wonderful frozen concoction that helped Jimmy Buffett hang on. Hey, wait a second—"Some people claim that there's a woman to blame, but I know it's my own damn fault." Shit, Jimmy Buffett cusses in that song too! No wonder I like it so much.

"Let's get after it," G.W. said, and boy, did we. Before I knew it, I was on drink number four, trying hard just to keep up with Claire and Pam. It was quite a relief to be there, compared to the stiff celebration that we'd attended earlier that afternoon. Everyone was catching a major buzz.

And then it happened:

Craig grabbed a pitcher full of those delicious margaritas and dropped the whole thing on the kitchen floor. It went everywhere. On people's shoes, on the cabinets, but mostly all over my sister Lisa's pants. She reached down and grabbed the pitcher off the floor. Luckily it was plastic and didn't shatter. She yelled to G.W. to turn the music off. He quickly shut off the Talking Heads because Lisa looked extremely pissed. I'd seen that look before and I knew the party was over.

"My husband has had too much to drink," she yelled, and the room got really quiet. She paused for effect. "And there's a good reason for that . . . Because we have an announcement to make: Craig and I are going to have a baby!"

The room erupted into cheers. I was jumping up and down like I'd just won the lottery. I was so happy that my little sister was going to have a kid. "Why'd you wait until now to say anything?!" I asked.

"Well, I didn't want to take any of the spotlight away from Sydney. This is her day."

"Let's get this party restarted," G.W. yelled, and put the music back on. I went out to our car and got the Khia CD. I asked G.W. to put it on, and before it started, I made an announcement.

"I'd like to dedicate this next tune to Craig and Lisa. This is how you got into the predicament that you're in right now!" We played "My Neck, My Back" five or six times in a row, and didn't stop cheering and toasting for the next several hours.

We finally stumbled out of Casa Mix around two in the morning.

The best thing that night was that Lisa was our designated driver. I rode with her as we made several trips back and forth to Crooked Oak Lane, taking our very intoxicated family home. We cranked "My Neck, My Back" and sang along the entire trip home.

"I can't believe you're playing this song in front of my twenty-one-year-old daughter," Rob yelled from the back seat.

"I'm sure Lindsay's heard profanity before, Rob."

"Not in a song," he said cracking up laughing.

It was such a great day and night. We had celebrated Sydney's First Holy Communion. We had gotten the wonderful news that Lisa and Craig were expecting their first child. And we had all become masters of singing the best profanity-laced song of all-time. It was the perfect ending to a perfect day.

But there's always a morning after. And when your kids are five and eight, it's usually a very early morning after. Boy, were we hurting. By seven thirty, we had a full house. My mom and dad stopped by to say goodbye before they drove back to Creedmoor. Claire's parents, Pam and Joe, came by to have breakfast and to take Sydney and Lucas to shop at Zany Brainy. I was really excited that the grandparents were taking the kids off our hands for a couple of hours.

"Just take our car. Lucas's car seat is already in it," I said.

We loaded the kids into the back seat, and Pam got in. I tossed Joe the car keys and he adjusted the rearview mirror and turned the ignition switch. Not only did it start the car, it started the music at volume 11.

"My neck, my back . . ."

"What the hell is that?" Joe barked at me as he fumbled to turn off the music.

"I don't know," I quickly responded. "This is your daughter's car."

Fifteen years later, I got a call from my sister Lisa. She said she was making dinner with her family and got a crick in her neck. She said she rubbed it and said out loud, "My neck . . ."

Craig giggled and quickly said, "My back . . ."

"Y'all are gross!" Emily, their fifteen-year-old daughter responded.

"Oh my God, how do you know that song?" Lisa asked.

"I don't know," she said, "I just know it."

I know how she knew it. I'm convinced Emily heard it for the first time on Cinco de Mayo fifteen years earlier. In utero.

That song is unforgettable. It'll never go out of style. It's the best damn song of all time.

Addendum

A couple of months before this book was published, my mom, who is seventy-seven years old, asked me to send her one of my stories, so she could get a sense of what the book was about. Naturally, I sent her this story. I didn't hear from her for a few days. But I did hear from my sister, Lisa. She asked me how Mama knew about the "My Neck, My Back" story. I told her that I'd sent it to her. "Well, that explains it," she said.

"Explains what?" I said.

"It explains why Mama was asking Emily to play that song for her."

"What did Emily say?" I asked.

"She said, 'Grandma, you don't need to hear that song,'" Lisa said.

"That's funny."

"And then she asked *me* to play it for her."

"What did you say?" I chuckled, imagining my mom prancing around her kitchen with her cane in one hand and some gluten-free potato chips in the other, belting out those raunchy lyrics.

"I said the same thing Emily said: 'Mama, you don't need to hear that song.' I'm not playing it for her. I sure don't want to be there when she starts singing it. If she's going to hear that song, she's going to hear it from you, David," Lisa said.

I guess I'm not the only one who isn't entirely comfortable talking about sex with my mom.

A couple days later, my mom called me and said that she really enjoyed the story and was looking forward to reading more. She told me that she had asked Emily and Lisa to play "My Neck, My Back," and they both flat-out refused to play it for her. They said she didn't need to hear that song. Mom said she told them both that married people, and couples, do all kinds of sexual things in a close relationship and that it is nothing to be ashamed of.

"Oh," I said.

"Well, I'm determined to hear that song," she said. "I've just had other things going on that have gotten in the way so far. I'm a busy woman. I have to watch *Jeopardy!* every night. I've learned a lot from that show. You never know, one night the category might be Music Lyric/Artist, and the Daily Double might come up, and Alex Trebek would say, 'Here's the clue . . . My neck, my back,' and the contestant wouldn't know the answer. But if *I* had heard the song, I would know."

Well, that's as good of a reason as any to hear it, I thought. So I emailed her the link to Khia's "My Neck, My Back" video on YouTube. She emailed me back ten minutes later: "I'm going to have a lot of fun with this. I can't wait to see Emily and Lisa." I'm sure by now she has memorized the lyrics and is working on a dance routine for their next visit.

THE CANINE CRAPPERER

I am convinced that I have seen more dogs poop than anyone on earth. I don't know what it is, but whenever I'm in the presence of a canine, nature seems to call at that exact moment, and the dog always answers with a big fat dump. I am not exaggerating.

I take our lab, Walter, out first thing each morning and he drops a deuce every time. He's not the least bit shy about it. You'd think he'd have the courtesy to hide behind a tree before he squats, but no, he poops right in plain view. It's almost as if he's proud of his production. "Hey look, Dave," he seems to say, "I just manufactured another solid Lincoln Log. Now feed me so I can make another."

But it's not just Walter. Each day on my drive to the office, I see at least one pooch assume the position. Shitting Shitzus. Dumping Dalmations. Crapping Collies. They all fertilize lawns as I drive by. It's not like I'm looking for them. Quite the contrary. I'm convinced they're looking for me. Yesterday, I made a point to keep my eyes only on the road. I was so focused on driving down Queens Road West that Heidi Klum could've jogged by and my head wouldn't have turned an inch. I almost made it to work without a single shit-sighting, when a lady walking her beagle crossed the crosswalk at the intersection of East and Camden. I am not BS-ing you; the beagle stopped and dropped right in the middle of the road. This Poopy Snoopy looked back at me and winked. I swear he did. What's even worse, his owner didn't even pick up the turd. So, when the light changed, I drove over it. I got to the office and it was stuck in the treads of my tire.

No! Don't poop now. Wait until Dave is watching.

You've heard of the Horse Whisperer? I am the Canine Crapperer.

Maybe dogs are just relaxed around me. That, or I literally scare the shit out of them. Whatever it is, it has long ceased being funny to me.

What is funny to me is seeing a cow piss.

When I was growing up, my Aunt Hallie had a funny saying. Whenever it looked like rain, she'd say, "There's a cloud coming up. That rain's fixing to come down like a cow pissing on a flat rock." Then she'd start laughing. And her laugh is so infectious that I couldn't help but start laughing too.

"Why is that so funny?" I asked her.

"Have you ever seen a cow piss?"

"No, can't say that I have," I said.

"Well, if you had, you'd think it was funny."

"Why?" I asked.

"Because piss comes out of a cow like water shooting out of a firehose. And it splatters all over everywhere. Especially if the cow is standing on a flat rock." Then she started cracking up again. So did I.

"Someday, David, I'm going to take you to see a cow piss."

Well, I think I was eleven years old when Aunt Hallie made that promise, and it was thirty years later when she actually fulfilled it. I'll never forget it. Claire, the kids and I had driven to Butner to visit Aunt Hallie. I think Sydney was about eight and Lucas was five. We were trying to think of something to do to pass the time with the kids, so Aunt Hallie suggested that we drive over to the farm town of Stem and see the cows. Sydney and Lucas were psyched. We all piled into our Passat wagon. Even Aunt Hallie's dog, Duchess, came along.

We parked our car near the gate of the cow pasture, where probably a hundred cows were grazing. They were black-and-white cows, just like the ones on Ben & Jerry's ice cream containers.

"They're Holsteins," Claire declared. She should know. Claire went to college in Burlington, Vermont, where Ben & Jerry started their ice cream empire.

There wasn't much for the cows to graze on in the field since it was mid-February and the temperature was in the mid-thirties. A couple of cows walked over to the fence right beside where we were standing. I think they were expecting us to feed them. Then it happened. One of the big girl cows started peeing. She wasn't just peeing. She was pissing.

"Look, Lucas! Look, David! Look, Sydney!" Aunt Hallie yelled, "That cow's pissing." And she started laughing. "It's pissing on a flat rock. Bah ha ha." Her laugh rang joyously through the chilly air. The more that cow pissed, the more Aunt Hallie laughed. "Bah ha ha."

Steam rose like a geyser when the cow piss hit the ground. Then a second cow started pissing. And then a third. Before we knew it there must have been fifty cows standing within twenty yards of us pissing and splattering and steaming up the whole field. The only thing louder than the piss hitting the ground was the symphony of our laughter. Lucas and Sydney were cracking up. I was crying I was guffawing so hard. Claire was cackling. She told me later that she almost peed in her pants. It was synchronized pissing on a flat rock.

After a couple of minutes, the downpour finally subsided. I looked at Aunt Hallie and asked, "Have you ever seen this happen before?"

"No, I've never seen anything like it," she said.

"Me either," I said. "I've never seen a cow piss before."

"Well, those cows must feel really comfortable around you, David," she said, and burst into laughter again.

Since the show was over and the kids were getting cold, we loaded up the car to head back to Aunt Hallie's house. I put the car in reverse, looked behind me, and started backing up.

"Wait, where's Duchess?" Aunt Hallie said, turning around and looking everywhere.

I put the car back in park and looked out the driver's side window, and there she was. Squatting by the fence of the cow pasture.

Taking a dump.

WALTER'S MEDICINE

Claire and I made a pact when we decided to have kids: no matter what happened, the two of us would always be number one. The kids would always be secondary to our relationship. We honored our pact religiously for twenty-eight years.

Then Walter came along, quickly becoming the number-one male in the Oakley household. The moment he arrived, I lost my status as the top dog with Claire.

Honestly, I brought this on myself. Walter is an adorable black lab. I gave him to Claire as a Christmas present. She had been wanting a dog since Syd and Lucas had left for college. I figured that she wanted another kid. What I failed to realize was that she was looking for my replacement.

I've accepted my new place in the hierarchy now—I love Walter. That doesn't mean that he doesn't annoy me from time to time. And by time to time, I mean daily. A couple of nights ago, Sydney was at our house because she and Claire were going on a mother-daughter ski trip early the next morning. I was going to stay at home and take care of Walter.

Regardless of the fact that I was a partner in successfully raising two kids from infants into their twenties, Claire regards my ability to take care of her dog by myself for a weekend as somewhere slightly below incapable.

While we were making dinner, Claire pointed at a little blue prescription bottle on the kitchen counter and said to me, "Dave,

Walter's medicine is right there on the counter. Remember to put it in his food. You need to crush the pill and sprinkle it over his food or he won't eat it."

"OK," I said as I set the table.

When we were finishing dinner, she petted Walter on the head and said, "Walter really needs his medicine to get better, Dave. It's over there on the counter. He gets one pill, and you need to crush it up and sprinkle it on his food."

"I know, Claire, I've been doing the routine for the last three days."

Three days earlier, Walter had eaten something in the backyard, or at least that was the hypothesis. I'd heard him crying in distress at five thirty in the morning. I sprang out of bed and raced into the den, but arrived a split second too late. Or right on time, if you subscribe to the theory that I'm always present for a dog-shitting event. Walter was midway through spraying explosive diarrhea all over. The crate. The wall. The carpet. And me. When I opened his crate, he sprinted to the door, leaving a trail of splattered shit on everything in his wake. After a night of drinking at Wooden Robot, cleaning dog shit was not how I wanted to start my day. So, believe me when I tell you, I was well aware of what kind and how much medicine Walter needed. I sure as hell didn't want to go through that again, so I damn well wasn't going to forget to give him his medicine while Claire and Sydney were gone.

An hour later, Claire looked up from watching *The Bachelor* and said to me, "Walter's medicine is on the counter. Don't forget to mash it up and put it on his food."

"That's the third time you've told me that. What, do you think I'm an idiot? The dog will be fine when you're gone."

"Well, you don't always listen."

Sydney looked up at me from the couch and grinned, obviously enjoying this loving interaction. "Dad, don't forget to give Walter his medicine."

"Wait, what? Who needs medicine?" I laughed and said, "I'm going to bed. I'll get up with you guys in the morning and say goodbye."

Before I left, I took a glance around the room and saw that there was only one thing on our kitchen counter: The little blue bottle of doggy diarrhea medicine.

I went to bed. The alarm went off at four forty-five, and Sydney requested the Uber. I helped them load their bags into the car and the two of them left on their ski trip. It was so early, Walter didn't even wake up.

I went back to bed, but I couldn't go back to sleep. Why? Because I was having flashbacks of cleaning dog shit. I had a choice: I could continue to lounge in bed and risk a repeat, or I could go let Walter out of his crate. I chose to not take the chance. I let Walter out. He scurried outside and did his business.

I grabbed his dog bowl and filled it with the finest non-grain fish-and-lamb performance dog food money can buy. Claire spares no expense when it comes to feeding her Wally-woo. I walked over to the counter to get the medicine, and it wasn't there. I blinked a couple of times to see a little clearer—after all, it was seven a.m., and I wasn't really awake. Still there was no medicine. *Wait, did they tell me it would be in the cabinet or something? Maybe in the refrigerator? In the closet?* Maybe I really wasn't listening to Claire last night. I looked everywhere, and I couldn't find it. Walter stared at me like *WTF, would you stop walking around like a dunce and just feed me?*

So, I did. I fed him and didn't give him any medicine. He gobbled it down in two seconds. He followed me back to the bedroom. Maybe the medicine was in a logical place. Like our medicine cabinet. Nope. Not in my closet. Not anywhere. I went back to the kitchen and the counter was still empty. No sign of the medicine.

My phone buzzed and it was a joint text from Claire and Syd. She sent their flight number and said that they had boarded their flight to

Dallas. I texted back, *Did you guys hide Walter's medicine?*

Claire quickly replied, *Ha, ha, very funny.*

Sydney chimed in, *It's on the counter, Dad. Don't you ever listen to Mom? LOL*

Claire texted back quickly, *The answer is "No." LOL*

I couldn't tell if they were messing with me or not. But I definitely couldn't let them know that I couldn't find Walter's medicine. Forget Walter: I would get unending shit from *them* forever. The text chain had been silent for about twenty minutes when Syd texted, *We're about to take off.*

Claire typed, *How's Walter?*

I responded, *Walter's fine. I gave him some Pepto-Bismol instead. Hahahaha. We'll text when we land.*

I took Walter to our office like we do every day. He's one of several office dogs and is right at home there. I started working. A couple hours later I got a phone call from Claire. They had landed in Dallas.

"Oh my God, you are not going to believe this. I just opened my purse to take my altitude sickness medicine, and I pulled out Walter's medicine. Can you believe that? I must have grabbed it this morning thinking it was my altitude medicine. I was so out of it this morning. Isn't that funny?"

"It's funny if you think having me look everywhere in the house for that stupid medicine is funny." Then I imitated Claire: "David, Walter's medicine will be on the counter. Don't forget to give it to him. I thought I'd lost my mind. Or that you guys were totally fucking with me and had hidden it."

"Calm down. Why didn't you just tell me you couldn't find it?

"I tried to, but you totally ignored me."

"You're always kidding around! We thought you were just joking. Why didn't you just say you couldn't find it?"

"Because you would have given me endless shit because I didn't listen or had forgotten the instructions you gave me last night," I said as I rubbed Walter's belly.

"Whatever. I'll call the vet and get them to fill a new prescription and you can pick it up this afternoon on your way home. It's not a big deal."

"OK, that works for me," I said, noting how forgiving Claire was of her own mistake. A mistake that would have been a big deal if anyone else had made it. If Sydney had put Walter's medicine in her purse, Claire's response would have been very different. That would have been a BIG deal. No, it would have been a gigantic deal. Claire would have cancelled Sydney's ski trip and booked her on the first flight back to Charlotte to personally return the medicine and apologize to her beloved Walter.

That evening, I got home and filled Walter's bowl again with his gourmet food. I looked on the counter for his medicine and it still wasn't there. *Damn it*, I thought, *I forgot to pick it up.* "Oh well, I'll pick it up tomorrow. He'll be fine," I said to myself.

Just then my phone rang, and it was Claire, aka Walter's watchdog. "How's Walter?"

See what I mean? Not a single question like, *Dave, how was your day?* It's always Walter, Walter, Walter . . .

"Oh, all he's doing is moping around. He's so sad that you're gone. I had to hide his pills," I said.

"Why?"

"He's on suicide watch. He's so depressed that you've abandoned him."

"Ha, ha. Did you remember to give him his medicine?"

"Of course," I lied without hesitation, knowing that honesty is not always the best policy when it comes to taking care of the precious one.

"Did you chop it up and mix it with his food?"

"No, I shoved it up his ass."

"Dave . . . did you give him his medicine?"

"Yes, he gobbled it down."

"Great. How was the vet?"

"Fine."

Then she asked a trick question. "How much did they charge you for it?"

I had no idea how much that fucking medicine costs. It could have been $10, $50, or $300. I had no clue. But in a split second I decided on my answer. "Nothing. They thought it was a funny story, so they gave it to us for free."

"Oh, they are so nice there."

The next morning, I remembered to stop at the vet. I asked for Walter's medicine, and the vet's assistant put it on the counter.

"That'll be $17."

That's not bad, I thought.

"Just swipe your card in the card reader," the assistant continued.

I pulled out my Visa card, but just before I swiped it, I changed my mind.

"Um, I'm going to pay cash."

Cash leaves no evidence. No paper trail. I guess that's why drug dealers always use cash. Even doggie drug dealers.

INDEPENDENCE DAY

Soon after Lucas was potty trained, I was talking with my dad, Sid, about how happy I was that I had changed my last poopy diaper. He agreed that it was quite a milestone, but it really wasn't the most liberating thing for a parent. "Just wait until they start bathing themselves. That's when you start to get your life back. That is freedom."

"Well, that's easy for you to say," I said. "You never changed our diapers. Mom did all the diaper changing when we were kids." Even though I'd hardly categorize my upbringing as traditional—I was the son of two semi-hippie artists after all—my mom still did most of the child-rearing and all of the housework.

"You're probably right," he acknowledged, laughing, "but every once in a while, I had to change you. But I always gave you and your sister a bath after dinner."

I didn't remember him doing that, either, but I humored him and let him continue.

"First of all, you and Lisa didn't like to take baths, so after a long day at work, I'd have to take you kicking and whining to the tub. Then I'd get you in the bath and start shampooing your hair, and some would get in your eyes and you'd start crying and I'd have to rinse it out and calm you down. Then you'd splash me and get my cigarettes wet. It happened almost every night."

My dad was a potter, so he didn't have to get dressed up to go to work. Every day, he wore a pair of jeans and what he considered a nice T-shirt. Nice, meaning that it had a pocket on the front to hold his filter-less Camels.

"So, you'd rather change a stinky peas-and-carrots-diarrhea diaper than bathe a baby?" I asked.

"Of course. Babies are happy when you change their diaper. They're pissed off when you make them take a bath."

I just chuckled.

"When you and Lisa were old enough that I could say, 'Go take a bath,' and you could do it on your own safely, it was the Fourth of July for me," he said.

"The Fourth of July?" I asked, totally confused.

"Independence Day. I had my life back."

I laughed. "So instead of trying to wash my hair and smoke a Camel at the same time, you could walk outside as soon as you finished your banana pudding and smoke in peace."

"That's right," he said as he lit up.

Sid was wrong about giving the kids a bath. I actually enjoyed it. If I hadn't given baths to my kids, I would have missed some of the most amazing conversations of my life. Like the time when Lucas was about four and was sitting in a tub full of Mr. Bubble. He looked up at me and said, "Daddy, I know where my brains are."

"You do? Where are they?" I answered in that kind of fake-sweet interested voice that parents speak to four-year-olds in.

"They're right here," he said as he pulled his penis out of the way and showed me his testicles. "This is my brain."

I summoned all my willpower to keep my laughter on the inside. "I thought your brain was in your head," I somehow managed to reply.

"No, Daddy, my brain is right here," he said, as he poked his ball sack.

Then I thought a thought that I'd never thought before: a scrotum really does look like a brain. A LOT like a brain.

"Well, Lucas, you might be right. You just might be right," I said as I walked over and opened the bathroom door. "I've got to get your towel." I grabbed his towel and buried my face in it and had a super silent laugh. No matter how funny what your kid says is, you can't laugh at them. If you do, they might not say something funny again.

But that sure didn't stop me from telling other people what he said. I told Claire's dad, who ran an oil and gas company in Manhattan, about it the next time I saw him.

"That kid's a freaking genius. Before you know it, he'll be CEO of a Fortune 500 company."

A couple of months later, I was giving Lucas another bath. It was the same scene as every night. I had finished washing his hair and he was playing with his boats and toys for a few minutes before I took him out and dried him off. He looked up and said, "Daddy, do you think that the Wicked Witch of the West has a green vagina?"

He looked at me like I really should know the answer. I have to give myself credit for thinking on my feet, even though I was on my knees at the edge of the bathtub.

"Well, Lucas, she has green hands and a green face, so I guess her body's green and that probably means that her vagina is green too."

"That's what I thought," he said.

As I dried him off, I said, "You know, Lucas, I'm not totally sure about the Wicked Witch. I think you should probably ask your mom and Aunt Mary Lou. They're girls. They'll know for sure."

He ran down the hall in his towel to the den. About fifteen seconds later it became clear that Claire and Mary Lou didn't follow the same protocol about not laughing at your kid's questions.

Years later, I realized that my dad was right. Even though I enjoyed those bathside chats with my kids, by the time they were old enough to bathe themselves, they weren't so funny anymore. And it freed up time for me to do the things that I really wanted to do after dinner. More important things.

Like walking through the neighborhood and watching the dogs shit.

BOTTLES UNDER THE BED

A s a parent, I'll be the first to admit that our kids get away with a lot. What I mean by that is that there are a lot of things they do that they don't tell us about. They're smart. And they are very good at hiding things from us. Especially when it comes to drinking.

That's why it's so satisfying when we bust them. If we happen to outsmart them to catch them, it's even better. It doesn't happen often, but when it does, it's cause for a celebration. Not an outward celebration, but an inward affirmation that as parents, we aren't as dumb as our kids think we are.

One especially gratifying example of this took place a few years ago when Sydney was a freshman at UNC, and Lucas was a sophomore in high school.

Claire and I were eating breakfast after dropping Lucas off at school. Claire's phone rang—it was Sydney. She had a sorority function that weekend and had left a certain pair of boots at home. She asked if Claire would go up upstairs to her bedroom and see if she could find them. Claire said she'd look for them in a little while.

Claire finished her oatmeal and disappeared upstairs. A few minutes later she walked back into the kitchen.

I looked up from my laptop. "Did you find them?"

"Oh, I found them," she said, "I also found these." She put two half-full bottles of wine and a half-full bottle of tequila on the kitchen counter.

"Where were they?" I asked.

"Under Sydney's bed!"

Two seconds later, Claire was on the phone with Sydney. "Not only did I find your boots, I found your booze."

I could only hear Claire's side of the conversation, but it was easy to get the gist of what was being said. "Two bottles of red wine and a bottle of tequila . . . Did you think we would never find it up there? Why didn't you take it back to Carolina with you? . . . Or is this your stash to drink when you're at home?" It was a full-on Claire grilling. She ended the conversation on a good note, though, probably because she was thrilled that she had busted Sydney. "Yes, I have your boots and I'll put them in the mail today. You should get them by Friday. OK, I love you, Syd. Bye."

"Well, what did she say?"

"She said she forgot that it was up there. It was from last summer," Claire said, massaging her temples.

"Oh, OK," I said, "Are you sure it's Sydney's booze?"

"Well, who else's would it be?"

"Maybe it's Lucas's," I ventured.

"Lucas is a sophomore in high school. He doesn't drink," Claire said.

"You never know. I was drinking when I was fifteen."

"Well, Sydney just said it was hers."

Claire was convinced that the wine and tequila belonged to Sydney. But I wasn't. That afternoon I did a little research. I looked up the two bottles of wine on the internet. The 2012 Gramercy Cellars Columbia Valley Cabernet Sauvignon retailed for $49. The 2011 Wynns Cabernet Sauvignon Black Label sold for $44. *Interesting*, I thought. This wine seems to be a little out of a college freshman's price range.

That evening, while Claire was teaching her yoga class, I decided to ask Lucas about the bottles. He was watching *Shark Tank* on TV. I sat down on the couch beside him. "Did Mom tell you that we found three bottles of alcohol under Sydney's bed this morning?"

"No," he said, not looking away from the TV.

"Yep, two bottles of wine and a bottle of tequila."

"Did you talk to Sydney about it?" he asked.

"Yes, Mom called her this morning and totally busted her. Syd said she forgot about them and that they were from last summer."

"Oh wow," said Lucas, the picture of nonchalance.

"It just seems weird to me. I drank when I was in high school, but I would never hide my alcohol under my bed. I would always hide my stuff in my sister Lisa's room. That way, if anyone found it, they would think it was Lisa's, not mine."

As Lucas sat there listening, I continued, "I just don't think Sydney would hide alcohol under her own bed. I think it might be somebody else's."

"Whose?"

I slid to the edge of the couch, turned and leaned toward him.

"I think it might be yours, Lucas."

"Mine?" Lucas answered incredulously, as his cheeks flushed to the color of a Robert Foley cabernet. For the first time he took his eyes off *Shark Tank* and looked at me.

"Is it yours?"

"No."

"OK, good. So you think it's Sydney's alcohol."

"I guess so. She said it was hers."

"Well, even though she said it was hers, I'm still not sure. I noticed something unusual about this wine. Let me show you." I went into the dining room and came back to the den with the two bottles of wine.

"Check out this wine. It's expensive. I looked them both up on the internet and they are almost $50 apiece. I don't think that's the kind of wine that college students buy. It seems like that's the kind of wine that wine aficionados drink. Your friend Connor's parents are really into wine, aren't they? So is your friend Catherine's mom, right? I wonder if they are missing any Gramercy Cellars Columbia Valley Cabernet or Wynns Cabernet Sauvignon Black Label from their houses. I'm going to give them a call and ask."

"I don't think you should do that."

"Oh really. Why? Because it's your wine?" Lucas just sat there and didn't say anything. "Do you have their numbers? I'm going to give them a call."

"I don't want to get my friends in trouble."

OK, I thought, *we have a breakthrough.*

"Look Lucas, if you will tell me it's yours, I won't call them."

"OK, it's mine," he said immediately, "Please don't call them!"

I felt like Andy Sipowicz on *NYPD Blue*. I had gotten the suspect to crack.

"OK, I'm not going to call them."

"Thank you," he said, and gave me the prayer-hands gesture.

"You should be very happy that your sister covered for you like that. Apparently, Sydney's got your back. And I'm really happy that you felt you could tell me the truth about it. So, I'm not going to ground you, I'm not going to punish you. But I will ask you to do one thing: You have to tell your mom that the alcohol is yours. How's that sound?"

"Not good."

I knew this was the most severe punishment I could have ever dealt out. Why? Because I knew she was going to be pissed. Not so much that the alcohol was his, but because I was right about it.

I was so happy that I had solved the case. I was sure that the kids would pull more stuff over on me in the future, but I had won this battle. It was a big victory. Kinda like winning my own Super Bowl.

Even if I never win another, I'll always have that championship ring.

A couple years later, when Lucas was a freshman in college, we were in the kitchen and I looked in the freezer to get a Paul Newman's pizza for dinner. I noticed that our bottle of Tito's was frozen solid. *That's odd*, I thought.

Lucas was sitting at the kitchen table. *Suspect number one!*

"How's your physics class was going?" I asked.

"Good," he replied.

"Have you guys studied things like the boiling point and freezing point of water yet?"

"Yeah," he said.

"Well what's the boiling point of water?"

"212 degrees Fahrenheit, or 100 degrees Celsius."

"What's the freezing point of water?"

"32 degrees Fahrenheit, or 0 degrees Celsius."

"OK good. You know your stuff." I said. "So, what's the freezing point of vodka?"

"Dad, vodka doesn't freeze," Lucas said, in his high-school-senior know-it-all way.

"Oh really?" I opened the door to the freezer and pulled out the bottle of Tito's.

"So why is this vodka frozen solid?"

Lucas immediately burst into laughter, which was not the reaction I was expecting.

"I guess someone replaced the vodka with water," he said. "That's hilarious."

"Was that someone you, Lucas?"

"Perhaps," he said.

An admission of guilt! Once again, I was quite impressed with my detective work. Lucas was guilty and we both knew it.

"Or maybe it was Miss Cathy," he said with a chuckle.

This crack made me start laughing too. Miss Cathy was a babysitter who'd stayed with Lucas and Sydney after school years before, back when they were in elementary school. She had a couple of interesting habits. Like falling asleep while the kids were watching TV. Or backing her car across our lawn when she would leave our house. We didn't really think that her behavior was that unusual for a seventy-something lady. She was just old, we thought.

Until one day, I noticed that our Tito's in the freezer had less vodka in it than I remembered it having. I asked Claire if she'd drunk any of the vodka, and she said no. I knew it wasn't Sydney or Lucas, so it had to be Miss Cathy. But I couldn't just accuse her of drinking on the job unless I did a little more investigating.

So I did something that I had seen on a TV show once. I made a small mark with a Sharpie on the bottle to denote how full it was with vodka. Miss Cathy came and stayed with the kids on Monday afternoon, and when she left, I checked the bottle. Sure enough, the vodka level in the bottle was one inch lower. I marked the bottle again, and on Tuesday evening I checked it again. It was another inch lower. This happened again on Wednesday. On Thursday, I met Miss Cathy at the house and confronted her about the disappearing spirits.

"How could you ever accuse me of that?" she asked. "Well, I never . . ."

"If it wasn't you, then who was it? Sydney? Lucas? One of the kids in the neighborhood? Either way, the vodka is disappearing on your watch. And since I've lost all trust in you now, I have to let you go."

"I've never been let go in my life. I had nothing to do with your gin or vodka or whatever it was. Goodbye," she said, and walked out the kitchen door, got in her car, and backed across our lawn.

Guilty as charged! Again, detective David has solved the mystery. I was so proud of myself for figuring it out that I bored our friends at dinner parties with the story for years.

But recently there has been a new development in the case.

Sydney and Lucas, who are now both of legal drinking age, told me last week that they never liked Miss Cathy as a babysitter. Which makes me wonder? Maybe they poured the vodka out each day just to get rid of her . . .

They're smart.

But not that smart.

Or are they?

Shit.

IF SOCCER HAD RAINOUTS

There's one difference between soccer and baseball: soccer games are never rained out. Some people may argue that this is one of the great things about soccer. I contend that this small distinction is what makes baseball a far superior sport. As a parent of kids who played both sports, I should know.

Our kids grew up playing sports. Sydney played soccer and Lucas played baseball. I loved going to their games and watching both of them play, especially on beautiful 72-degree afternoons. You might say I'm truly a fair-weather fan. But I even enjoyed watching when it was 38 and overcast. I'm just not a fan of watching them play in the rain. Oh wait, I've only seen soccer in the rain.

Because baseball doesn't happen when it precipitates. Baseball umpires are often accused of being blind, but they all can see rain falling and have the sense to literally come in out of the rain and wait for a nice day to play. Or at least a nicer day for the parents to sit on those hard-ass wet metal bleachers.

Having two kids who are active in team sports means that sometimes the game times conflict. Claire and I oftentimes had to divide and conquer. I normally would go with Lucas to his baseball game, and Claire would take Sydney to soccer. Unless, of course, it was raining. Then there was only one game. And on those occasions, we normally both would go to the soccer game. Unless it was a really early game. In that case, I would let Claire sleep in. Not that I was being super nice or anything; I'm just an early riser.

One March weekend, Sydney's club soccer team, Charlotte United Green, was in a tournament in Matthews. The night before the tournament, Claire and I watched the weather report on WCNC at eleven. Meteorologist Brad Panovich told us to brace for strong winds and heavy rain throughout the night and continuing through Saturday afternoon. Flash flood warnings were in effect, but luckily temperatures were going to stay above freezing. Lucky us.

Sydney's first game was at eight o'clock on Saturday morning. Which meant the girls had to be at the field at seven for warm-ups. Which meant Syd and I would have to leave the house at six thirty. Which meant that we would have to get up at six. Which meant that we would have to set the alarm for five forty-five, because for some reason, I have a hard time enthusiastically jumping out of bed to stand in the rain for three hours.

Sydney and I made it to the fields on time for warm-ups. What a stupid name, "warm-ups." We were warm in the car. Cool-downs started as soon as we stepped outside. For once, the weatherman was right. It was truly a blustery, miserable day. A day where parents of baseball players all over Charlotte were still snug in bed, resting comfortably, knowing that their games had been sensibly canceled.

I stayed in the car until game time and then walked over to watch. Or should I say, tried to watch. It was foggy, and the rain was coming down so hard I could barely tell which players were which. But I could hear the splashing and the mud flying as they ran by. This went on for what seemed like hours, but I'm told it was actually only ninety minutes. The game ended the way it began: in a scoreless tie.

Afterward, Sydney walked up to me, drenched from head to toe. I looked at her shivering in her number-8 jersey and seriously questioned my sanity. Can you imagine on a cold, windy, rainy day, any parent looking out the window and saying to their kids, "Hey, look at that rain coming down sideways. You children go outside and play"?

And even if they did, what parent would go stand outside and watch them play?

"Dad, we're going to go jump and splash around in the ditch by the road. Wanna come outside and watch?"

"Sure, that sounds like fun. Mom, come with me, let's watch Sydney and her friends catch pneumonia together." But that's what you do with soccer. And not only that, we pay Charlotte United Football Club for the privilege.

A couple of weeks later, we had another divide-and-conquer day. Sydney had a soccer game in Asheville and Lucas had a baseball game here in Charlotte. Both games were on Sunday afternoon at two. The weather was kind of iffy. It could have rained all day, or it could have cleared up and been a perfect day for baseball. It was hard to tell. A light drizzle was falling when Claire and Syd left for Asheville around eleven. Soon after they left, Lucas said to me, "Do you think we'll play today?'

"I'm not sure. Let me check my email," I said. A message from Larry Brown, the South Park baseball commissioner, had just come in. All games at Carmel fields had been canceled for the afternoon.

A sly smile crept across my face. This time it was Claire who was going to be standing on a soccer sideline in the pouring rain. And I was going to be sitting on the couch watching *Austin Powers: International Man of Mystery* with Lucas.

Baseball rocks!

Lucas and I were going to get to hang out around the house doing what guys do best. Be guys. We popped some popcorn in our illegal microwave, and opened a bag of chips and a can of Doritos dip. I grabbed a Budweiser for myself, and an IBC root beer for Lucas. It was just the two of us—until we were halfway through the movie.

That's when we heard the knocking on the door. At least that's what I thought it was at first. But then I realized that the knocking wasn't coming from the door. And it wasn't really a knocking, it was a tapping. Like *tap . . . tap . . . tap*. And then *tap . . . tap . . . tap . . .* again. It was coming from the wall outside the den.

"It's a woodpecker!" Lucas exclaimed.

I left my perch on the couch and walked over to the window. *Tap . . . tap . . . tap . . .* I jumped, waved, and clapped my hands, and the bird flew away.

"That takes care of that," I said as I plopped back down. No sooner had my ass hit the couch than the tapping started again.

"Damn, that's a pesky little pecker," I said, amused at the double meaning that went over nine-year-old Lucas's head. "Let's just ignore him. Eventually he'll stop."

I was wrong. The tapping continued. I turned up the volume on the movie and tried to ignore it. But the freaking woodpecker was tapping like he was getting paid per tap. Lucas then looked at me and said, "I can take care of the woodpecker. I'll hit him with a rock."

"OK, Lucas, you do that," I said just as the Fembots confronted Austin Powers. Austin starts dancing and the Fembots find him irresistible and they start exploding. This scene cracks me up. *This has to be one of the funniest scenes in the history of movies*, I thought. Then I saw Lucas from the corner of my eye. He was standing outside under the dogwood tree with a rock in his hand, staring intently at what I presumed was the woodpecker. A second later, he went into a full baseball pitcher's wind-up. It happened quickly, but it was so surreal that it really felt like it was in slow motion. Lucas kicked his leg up and hurled the rock toward the bird. It was a perfect shot. If he had been aiming at me. The rock crashed through the window, went right by my head, and landed in the kitchen.

"Lucas, what the hell are you doing?" I screamed through the broken window. I jumped off the couch and sprinted outside, yelling so loud that I'm surprised Claire didn't hear me in Asheville. When I got to him, Lucas was crouched on the ground, knowing that he was in super big trouble. I just grabbed him and gave him the biggest hug.

"Holy shit, Lucas, we're in big trouble," I said. I started laughing at how absurd the situation was. "I told you to throw the rock. I gave you permission. So it's actually my fault." I was so engrossed in the movie that I essentially had told him that his plan to throw a rock at the woodpecker was OK. Truthfully, I thought he had better aim than that.

Lucas then asked a very astute question. "Do you think we could fix it before Mom gets home?"

Maybe we could have if it had been any other day of the week. But it was Sunday afternoon, and nothing was open. So, we got some duct tape out and taped it up to keep the wind, the rain, and the woodpecker out.

We went back inside and watched the rest of the movie. It wasn't quite as funny anymore. We knew were in trouble. We spent the rest of the afternoon waiting for Claire and Sydney to get home.

That afternoon I realized a couple of things. One, Lucas was right. He said he would take care of the tapping. He did. After his throw, the woodpecker was never heard from again.

And two, if soccer had rainouts, Claire would have been home, and that window never would have been broken.

LITTLE LEAGUE

I started coaching Little League as a way for me to bond with Lucas. And bond we did. From the time he was seven years old until five years later, when Lucas finally told me that he actually hated baseball, we spent each spring and fall on the baseball field together. He still jokes to this day about how I forced him to play baseball. *Whatever, Lucas.*

Now that I think about it, I'm sure it wasn't easy for Lucas to tell his baseball-crazed father that he didn't want to play anymore. But at least he did it with style.

Lucas was twelve, and the spring season was the last season he was eligible to play Little League. We were on the way to Dick's Sporting Goods to buy new bat for the upcoming season when he broke the news to me.

"Dad, I don't want to play baseball this spring. I'm going to play tennis instead."

"Why?" I said looking at him in the rearview mirror.

"Baseball is boring. I hate it."

"Yeah, but you're one of the best hitters in the league. You like hitting, don't you?"

"Yeah, but in baseball I only get to hit four times a game. In tennis, I get to hit every four seconds."

I mean, how could I argue with that? So that's how Lucas's baseball playing days ended. And more importantly, how my coaching career came to an end.

But what a glorious coaching career it had been.

I coached the Pirates. The South Park Pirates. I met Russ Green-field and Greg Negus, who co-coached with me and have since become lifelong friends. It was an amazing experience, one I wouldn't trade for anything in the world.

Of course, all coaching comes with its share of other people second-guessing your decisions. And it wasn't always the other parents. Sometimes I'd have my reasoning questioned by a ten-year-old.

"Coach, why am I batting last?" Wesley said to me with tears welling up in his eyes. He'd just read the batting order that I had posted on the dugout wall.

I struck a diplomatic tone. "It's the batting order that I believe gives us the best chance to win."

"But coach, I'm an All-Star."

Technically, he was right. Wesley was an All-Star. But he was an All-Star because the District All-Star tournament had fallen on the Fourth of July weekend that year, and Wesley's family was one of the few that weren't on vacation. Wesley was added to the team at the last minute because we didn't have anyone else to play. Truthfully, he was lucky to even be on a regular team. He couldn't hit. He couldn't catch. He couldn't throw.

But it turned out he *could* run. Before I could get another word out, he burst into tears and sprinted out of the dugout, ran over the pitcher's mound, across second base, all the way across the field and climbed over the center-field wall, crying the whole way. He didn't stop until he climbed into the back seat of his parents' BMW.

Now I had a dilemma. Did I go chasing after the worst player in the league and bring him back and keep him in our lineup, which assured us of an out every time he came to the plate, or did I just let him go?

What do you think I did? I let him go. I smiled to myself because I realized that what I said to Wesley was true. Putting him last in the batting order did give us the best chance of winning. Especially now that he ran off and wasn't playing. It was one of my more brilliant coaching moves of the season.

The more I coached, the more obsessed with Little League I became. I loved every minute of it. Except the losing. That part I couldn't stand.

But winning at all costs is not what Little League is all about. It's about sportsmanship. It's about being part of a team. It's about having fun. It's not whether you win or lose, it's how you play the game. I adhered to that philosophy every season that I coached. Or at least every regular season. But once the playoffs started, all that feel-good shit went right out the window.

When playoff time rolled around, I would do anything to get a W. Even cheat. Not Houston Astros–level cheating, mind you. Just little theatrics that could be employed to give us an advantage. Sure, they would get our team fired up to win. But they would also deflate and distract our opponents. Our first game was against the Braves, who had a better record than ours in the regular season, and were definitely the favorites to win against the 3-9 Pirates. Until the night before the game, when Claire and I hatched an idea.

"I need something to fire the boys up for the game," I said.

"Like what?"

"I don't know, maybe some sort of *Win One for the Gipper* speech."

"Don't think that'll work," Claire said.

"Why not?"

"The boys don't really listen to you anyway. How about a mascot? Like Sir Purr, the Panthers' mascot. Or Hugo the Hornet."

I sat there for a second and didn't say anything. I looked past Claire to a framed photo in the den of her dressed as a clown. Then I said the words that every husband says to his wife at some point in their relationship.

"Will you dress up as a pirate?"

"Me?"

"Yeah, you were a great clown. You'd be an even better pirate! I've got a Roberto Clemente Pirates jersey you could wear."

"Yeah, but they'll know it's me."

"Yeah, that's true."

"But if I wore makeup, and a wig, and a beard . . ." Claire said. "C'mon, let's go!"

"Where?"

"Morris Costumes. I'm going to be a pirate tomorrow."

Morris Costumes is an institution in Charlotte. It's the place where everyone goes to get their Halloween costumes, but it's open year-round.

An hour later, we returned home with a long, black curly wig, a flowing black beard, big hoop earrings, a traditional tri-corner pirate hat, purple pirate trousers, black swashbuckler boots with a shiny gold buckle, and long plastic silver sword. And last but not least, an eye patch. In other words, the best pirate mascot costume ever.

Our first playoff game was at eight o'clock Saturday morning. We went through batting practice and infield warm-ups just like we did for every regular-season game. But instead of giving them a little pep talk in the dugout before the game started, I asked the boys to follow Coach Negus and Coach Greenfield to the storage shed right beyond the outfield wall. We gathered behind the shed, and I told them I had invited a special guest to talk with them. On cue, the door to the storage shed burst open, and out jumped Claire in full pirate regalia.

"Ahhrrrrrgggggghhhh, maties!!" she yelled.

The team looked on in stunned silence for about two seconds, then Matt Myers, a kid who wore Power Rangers boxers that were plainly visible under his white uniform pants, yelled, "We. Are. Pirates!" The rest of the boys started cheering and laughing like crazy.

"Ahrrrrrrrrrrr ... you ready for the playoffs?" she screamed.

"Yes," the boys responded in unison.

"Ahrrrrrrrrrr ... you ready to win?"

"Yessssssss!"

"That's right! Now everyone put your hands in here," Claire said. "You know what the Pirates are going to do today? We're going to kick booty ... kick booty ... kick booty ..."

The boys started chanting with her. "Kick booty ... kick booty ... kick booty ..."

Claire raised her sword skyward and yelled, "This game is ours, Pirates! Let's take it! Follow me!"

She started sprinting across the outfield carrying a skull-and-crossbones pirate flag with twelve ten-year-old Pirates screaming behind her. She ran straight for third base and paraded right in front of the Braves dugout, brandishing her sword and shouting at the shocked, gape-mouthed Braves, "You're going down today, you snaggle-toothed scalawags! You don't have a chance."

As soon as I went out to coach third base in the first inning, I was reminded once again that Claire is brilliant. That's when I heard one of the Braves whine dejectedly to their coach, "Coach Cooper, how come our team doesn't have a mascot?"

We won 9–2.

Later that afternoon, we were set to play the Yankees, who had just defeated the Cardinals. The Yankees' coach came over to me and said his team wasn't going to play us today because they were too tired, and they had homework to get done.

Coach Bruno was *that* coach. You know, the one who would yell at and belittle his players for making mistakes to their faces. (Unlike the rest of us, who swallowed our true feelings of contempt while we tried to encourage the little brats every time they made an error.)

Plus, the man would do his business inside the port-a-john beside the field. Literally do his business. He would call his coworkers on his cell phone and yell at them between innings for not making their sales numbers, thinking that the port-a-john was some sort of cone of silence where no one outside could hear him. It scared me, so I know it must have scared his players.

"Too tired?" I said to him. "We played at eight o'clock this morning and have been here all day waiting for your game to be done."

"Well, you understand, then. Your boys are tired too."

"No, the Pirates aren't tired. We're scheduled to play now, and we're ready to play."

"I'd rather play tomorrow."

I knew why he wanted to play tomorrow, and it had nothing to do with them being tired. It had to do with a Little League rule that if a pitcher pitches more than three innings, he can't pitch again for twenty-four hours. Coach Bruno's son Donald had pitched the game against the Cardinals, so he wouldn't be eligible to pitch against us. He was the only good pitcher the Yankees had.

We ended it up taking it to the league commissioner, who said "If both teams are there, you will play the game." I tried not to gloat as the kids took the field.

Coach Bruno had been right about one thing, though. His team was tired. The Pirates clobbered them, 12–0.

Next up, the Orioles in the championship game, Monday evening. All day Sunday, that was all I could think about. I thought we had a pretty darn good chance of winning the title. We hadn't used our best pitcher so he'd be available to start against the Orioles. Claire, the Pirates' mascot, was ready for action. I picked up the phone and started calling the players' parents to remind them that the game time was Monday at five o'clock. When I got to Wesley's name, I paused. *What if I tell his parents the game is at seven? Then when he shows up, the Pirates will already be champions.* What a fantastic idea!

On the way to the game, I was listening to WFNZ, Charlotte's sports talk radio station. I couldn't believe my ears when Mark Packer, the Packman, started talking about our game. "In about an hour, the championship game of South Park Little League will take place. It's a rematch of the 1971 World Series: the Orioles against the Pirates. If you are out and about, you should stop by Carmel Field. Admission is free."

Finally, it was game time. Our ace, Jimmy Bristol, was well-rested and ready to pitch. Jimmy was a rocket-armed lefty who threw about 85 mph. In other words, he threw smoke. I watched the Orioles taking batting practice in the batting cage before the game. Coach Norris was throwing his hardest to them to get his team ready to face Jimmy. The Orioles were well prepared to step into the batter's box against a fireballer.

That's when I had an idea. Coach Negus and Coach Greenfield agreed that it was risky, but worth a shot. Instead of starting Jimmy, we decided to let Simon Jones pitch. Simon was a blooper ball pitcher. He threw junk. His fastest pitch was maybe half as hard as Jimmy threw, but he had excellent control, meaning he didn't walk many people. When Simon took the mound for the first inning, Coach Norris looked over at me like I had lost my mind. Why in the world wasn't I pitching our best pitcher in the championship game?

Coach Norris had coached his Orioles to start swinging the bat the moment the ball left the Jimmy's hand. That way, their bat would be over the plate when the pitch came across. And maybe, just maybe they could make contact with the ball. But Simon threw the ball so slowly that the batters had already taken a full swing before the ball was halfway to the plate. Their timing was totally off. The Oriole hitters were swinging so far in front Simon's pitches that he was nearly unhittable.

I kept Simon in the game until the bottom of the sixth inning. We had a 4–2 lead when I sent Jimmy Bristol in to close out the game and bring the championship to the Pirates. Jimmy took the mound and struck out the first Oriole batter on three pitches. We were two outs from the trophy. The next guy fouled one pitch off and swung and missed the next two. Two down and we were on the verge of winning it all.

The next batter swung hard on the first pitch and weakly popped the ball up high in the air toward third base. Matt Myers, who was playing third, yelled, "I got it, I got it," and I watched the lazy pop fly fall harmlessly into Matt's glove.

That's it! We won it, we won it! My arms raised skyward in exultation, a rock-'n'-roll symphony orchestra exploded in my head, with Queen's Freddie Mercury crooning, *We are the champions, my friend.*

It was the best two seconds of my life.

Then I saw the ball bounce right off Matt's glove and fall to the ground. *Fuck.*

The game should have been over, but now the Orioles had new life, and I was overcome by a heavy dread that things had just taken a weird turn for the worse. They were still two runs down with two outs in the last inning, but the next hit went up the middle for a single. Jimmy walked the next batter, and up to the plate came Phillip Bullock, by far the best player in the league.

On Jimmy's first pitch, Phillip swung a little late, but still hit a towering fly ball to right field. The ball was heading straight toward Wesley.

Yes, that Wesley. What? You didn't really think I'd gone through with the plan to tell Wesley's parents the game started at seven, did you? Even *I* wouldn't stoop that low. I had definitely thought about it. All Sunday afternoon, in fact. But ultimately, I'd decided not to do it.

Wesley was playing deep on the warning track and didn't have to move an inch. He held his glove up in front of him, and somehow, some way the ball hit him right smack in the chest. The ball caromed toward the fence in the corner of the field. Wesley just stood there rubbing his chest. Our center-fielder chased the ball down in foul territory and fired it back into the infield just as Phillip was crossing home plate with the winning run. We had lost the championship on two errors in the last inning.

The Orioles were jumping around and celebrating like they had won the biggest game of their lives. Because they had. I wanted so badly to win that game. On the inside, I was crushed. On the outside, I kept it together. I went over and congratulated the Orioles and Coach Norris.

Before you knew it, I was in the trophy presentation, fake smiling as we were presented with our runners-up trophies. I wasn't mad at Wesley for missing the ball in the outfield. It was a tough play. And besides, he hadn't caught a ball all season. Even in practice. But Matt Myers? How had he missed that ball? My Aunt Hallie could've caught that pop-up with one of her rose-pruning gloves.

I told my team how proud I was of them and that even though they didn't win the game, they would always be winners in my eyes.

But I was lying.

I don't like losing. Let me rephrase that. I HATE losing. I'm not a bad sport; I always try to say the right thing after a defeat, like "good game." OK, there was that one time that I shot the bird at the other team after a tough bocce defeat, but that was an anomaly. Whether it's a Ping-Pong game or a cornhole match, outwardly I remain composed, but on the inside, I'm torn to shreds. It takes me a while to get over a loss—whether I played in the game or not.

I was depressed for weeks after the Panthers lost Super Bowl 50 to the Broncos. I was convinced that the game was fixed. Even the Falcons blowing a 28–3 lead in Super Bowl 51 didn't make me feel better. Oh, don't get me wrong, I was thrilled that the Falcons choked, but it still didn't bring a Super Bowl title to Charlotte.

When the Tar Heels lost to Villanova in the NCAA Finals in 2016, I was crushed. Marcus Paige hit a three-pointer for UNC to tie the game with four seconds left. But Kris Jenkins for Villanova hit a thirty-two-foot prayer at the buzzer to win the game for the Wildcats. I was devastated. I just kept seeing that play over and over in my mind for almost a whole year—until the Tar Heels won it all in 2017.

The agony of defeat is brutal. I don't know if I'll ever get over the Pirates losing to the Orioles in that Little League championship game. It's way worse than any Panthers loss or Tar Heel defeat. Why? Because those teams will always have a chance to play each other again the following season, but my Pirates will never get another chance to beat the Orioles.

A few months ago, I went to Sports Authority to do some last-minute Christmas shopping. I picked up a package of Ping-Pong balls and a new pair of sneakers for myself. Then I headed for the checkout. While I was standing in line looking at baseball cards, I heard a familiar voice, though it was much deeper than the last time I'd heard it.

"Coach Oakley, what's up?"

I looked up and saw Matt Myers. He was grinning like I imagined he'd grinned when his mom gave him his first pair of Power Rangers boxer shorts. My mouth dropped open in shock.

"So good to see you, Coach. How ya been?"

I couldn't believe it was Matt. He was all grown up. He was probably six foot three.

"Matt Myers!" I said, "What are you doing here?"

"I'm working over the holiday for some extra spending money. I'm a senior now at Boston College." I wondered if he knew Bill Buckner. (Buckner was the player for the Boston Red Sox who let an easy ground ball go through his legs, costing them the 1986 World Series.)

"Wow, that's great, Matt," I felt like we were holding up the line, but I didn't care and asked the man behind me to take a picture. I said to the man, "I used to be his Little League coach."

"We were pretty good, Coach Oakley."

"Yeah, we had some pretty good teams."

"I'll never forget winning that championship," Matt exclaimed.

I opened my mouth to correct him, but before I could sputter out the sad truth, he looked at the man behind me and said, "And we had a mascot. A PIRATE mascot!" Matt looked back at me. "By the way, Coach Oakley, I'm giving you the 30 percent coach's discount on your shoes."

"But—but I'm not coaching anymore, Matt."

"That doesn't matter to me. I'm giving it to you anyway, because of all the life lessons I learned playing for you."

I didn't know what to say. I just said, "Thank you," and walked out of the store wondering if what had just happened had actually happened. It hit me hard that Matt really thought we had won the championship.

Holy moly. Maybe that championship game against the Orioles really *didn't* matter. Maybe it's *true* that it's not whether you win or lose, it's how you play the game. There was no denying the game was fun. A lot of fun. We played it with Pirate spirit and Pirate gusto. We had a mascot. And that's what Matt remembered.

Maybe we really *were* champions.

Oh, bullshit.

Matt Myers dropped that pop-up. And I've got the second-place trophy to prove it.

THE PIRATE FLAG

Even though I was crushed by that loss in the championship game, I still have great memories from coaching Little League. Coaching the Pirates with my friend Greg Negus was some of the most fun I've had as a dad. But not all the fun happened on the field. One of my favorite Pirate adventures actually took place on a beach, five years after my coaching career ended. It confirmed to me something that I actually already knew: Coach Negus and I are Pirates for life.

It had been raining for three straight days. Just what you don't want when you're on a week-long vacation at Bald Head Island. Claire, the kids, and I had rented a cottage at this beautiful destination off the coast of North Carolina with our good friends Peg and Greg and their kids. It was late afternoon, and we were all getting a little stir-crazy, when Greg looked at the weather app on his phone and said, "It looks like it's going to stop raining in about twenty minutes. Anyone want to take the golf cart to the beach?"

"I'm in," I said.

"Maybe we can actually see a sunset," Peg said. The kids were engrossed in an *American Horror Story* marathon and couldn't be bothered to leave the couch. Before you knew it, the four of us adults were in a golf cart, thrilled to be out of the house and away from the kids, splashing through the mud puddles and laughing all the way to the beach.

When we arrived, the sun was starting to peek out from behind the clouds and the sand was still wet and pocked by the heavy raindrops. We started walking toward the water. There wasn't a soul on the beach. But there was one thing there that was out of the ordinary. About a hundred yards in front of us, in the middle of this deserted stretch of sand, was a flag. It was mounted on a wooden pole stuck in the sand.

"Is that what I think it is?" I asked Greg.

He squinted, and through giddy laughter he asked, "Is that a pirate flag?"

"It's a fucking pirate flag!" I exclaimed, and we took off running toward the flag. I grabbed the pole and pulled it up out of the sand and started waving it widely back and forth. "This is our beach now, motherfuckers. This is not Blackbeard's territory anymore. Now it's ruled by new pirates, the South Park Pirates." Greg and I ran a lap around Claire and Peg, who were carrying the beach chairs and the cooler, and then turned and sprinted toward the water, hooting and hollering the whole way, carrying the flag in all its glory. When we got to the water's edge, I planted the flag in the sand and shouted, "I claim this land for the South Park Pirates."

Of all the flags we could have found on that beach, nothing could have been more perfect than a pirate flag for Greg and me. Nothing. Had it been a Confederate flag, or a Trump 2016 flag or some shit like that, I wouldn't have touched it with a ten-foot pole. Even if it were a good ol' American flag, I wouldn't have grabbed it; I would have let it stand proudly in its place. But it was a pirate flag and we were Pirates, damn it! It was our flag. Greg and I were Coach Negus and Coach Oakley, the best Little League baseball coaches in the history of Little League!

Surely it was a sign from above that we were supposed to be there. The pirate gods were beckoning to Greg and me. The clouds had parted, the rain had stopped, the sun was shining, and we had found a Pirate flag. A crappy day had become perfect.

Pirates gonna be pirates.

We set up our chairs by the water's edge in front of the flag. Greg, Claire, and I jumped into the water and started swimming and floating around, laughing at how crazy it was that we had discovered a pirate flag. Peg sat down in the chair by the cooler and opened a bottle of wine. She raised her glass and waved to us in the water.

About twenty minutes later, I looked past Peg on the beach, and way in the distance I saw a group of young boys. They were gathered together with sticks or something in their hands. Suddenly they started running full steam toward the water. As they got closer, I could see that they weren't carrying sticks. They were carrying shovels. *That's kinda odd,* I thought, as I floated. *Bummer, these kids are about to jump in the water near us, and our tranquil swim is going to be interrupted.* But they didn't jump in the water. They had no interest in swimming. They weren't even wearing bathing suits. They were all dressed as pirates.

The boys stopped right behind Peg's chair and started digging maniacally. Peg didn't see or hear them over the roar of the waves, but as soon as they started throwing sand all over her, she noticed.

"Boys, watch the pinot grigio, watch the pinot grigio!" Peg yelled, covering her wine with her hand. "What the hell are you doing?"

"We're digging for treasure," one of the boys said.

"Well, dig somewhere else," Peg yelled. Another shovel full of sand hit her in the chest.

"No, this is where the treasure is," one of the boys said. "It's buried under the pirate flag."

We scrambled out of the water as fast as we could to try to protect Peg from this gaggle of beach buccaneers. Just then, I saw two of what I guessed were the boys' fathers running up the beach toward us. They didn't look happy. *Uh-oh. Maybe this wasn't a random pirate flag.*

"How did this flag get over here?" the first man yelled as he stormed up in the official uniform of Bald Head Island: matching Polo shirt and swim shorts.

"I moved it over here," I said.

"YOU stole the flag?"

"I didn't steal it. I thought someone had abandoned it."

"Who gave you the right to move it over here?" he said, his voice quivering with rage. Clearly this man had spent too many rainy days inside with his kids, and this had pushed him over the edge. He was furious.

"We coach a Little League teamed named the Pirates, and it's a pirate flag, and no one was out here. So I claimed it. That's what pirates do."

"Well, you just ruined my son's eighth birthday party."

"What? How did I ruin it?"

"His grandfather came out here earlier and buried a treasure under the pirate flag. Do you see how big this beach is?" he said, gesturing to the seven-mile-wide beach. "We'll never find it now."

"Oh man, I'm really sorry. I'll help you find it."

"We don't need any help from *you*," he practically spat. "You've already helped enough."

The father plucked the flag up from the sand and said, "Let's go, boys."

As the pirates stormed off in search of their elusive treasure, Greg, a true pirate who never passes up a chance to get a good dig in, said to me in his best Forrest Gump voice, just loud enough for that dad to hear him, "Sorry we ruined your pirate party."

"What'd you say?" the dad turned back to him and growled.

"He said, 'Good luck with your pirate party,'" I said, and waved to him.

Greg, Peg, Claire, and I walked back to our beach chairs. We turned them around and put our backs to the water. For the next hour or so until sunset, we watched those pint-sized pirates trudge back and forth across the vast expanse of sand, selecting spots to futilely dig for their buried treasure.

Did they ever find it? I don't know. But we found something to laugh about for the rest of the trip.

VEGAS ID

The National Parks in Utah are amazing. Zion, Bryce Canyon, and Arches are some of the most beautiful spots in the world. A couple of years ago, I used the allure of these natural beauties to trick my family into going to Las Vegas.

"I've been doing a lot of research on hiking out West, and I've come up with a family vacation plan," I told Claire as we were having dinner on our porch.

"Wait. You have a plan?" Claire said, insinuating that I never plan anything. She's actually right. I'm not a natural planner. I'm much more of a go-with-the-flow type. But there is one thing that I do plan: trips to Las Vegas.

"Yeah I've got a plan. A great plan. How does a National Park tour of Utah sound? We'll spend three days at Zion National Park. We'll hike the Zion Narrows, which is a riverbed that gets narrower and narrower, and at the end you're in a river looking up at 100-foot-tall canyon walls. Then we'll hike Angels Landing, one of the most challenging hikes in the West. Then we'll drive to Bryce Canyon, which I'm told is kinda like the Grand Canyon, only easier to get around in. We can ride horses through the canyon. And lastly, we'll go to Arches National Park, which you already know."

I knew Arches would be the clincher. Claire and I had camped at Arches together twenty years before, and it's one of her favorite places in the world.

"Oh, I love Arches," she said.

"Me too. I think the kids will love it too."

"How do we get there?"

"Well, we fly," I said, and smiled when Claire rolled her eyes.

"I know that, but where do we fly into? Salt Lake City?"

"We could, but that's way up in the northern part of Utah. It would be a lot more driving. We should fly into Vegas."

Claire snorted. "Vegas? Oh, I get it."

"What? It's about convenience. It's the closest airport to the National Parks. Zion is a six-hour drive from Salt Lake. It's only two hours from Vegas."

"So, when do you want to do this 'National Park' trip?" Claire asked, making air quotes with her fingers.

"The first week of August. We'll fly out Friday after work, get to Las Vegas in time for dinner, and maybe play a little blackjack, and then we'll head out to Zion first thing Saturday morning. We'll spend the next week in southern Utah, then come back to Vegas the next Friday night."

"Then we'll fly home Saturday morning, right?"

"I was thinking we'd fly home on Sunday."

"Two nights in Vegas?"

"Yeah. We will have just hiked for a week. You'll want to crawl into a nice comfy resort bed, maybe get a massage and chill for a while. It's the perfect plan."

"What are the kids gonna do? They can't gamble. Well, I guess Sydney can, but Lucas isn't twenty-one yet."

"I don't know. Watch TV? We could all go see a show Saturday night. Maybe the Beatles *Love* show? And maybe on Saturday we could go to the Neon Museum."

"I'll look into it and make a plan," said Claire, the natural planner.

I just smiled, because hooray! We were going to Vegas. Twice, actually.

Fast-forward three months.

We've just spent the last seven days in Zion, Bryce Canyon, and Arches National Parks. And we've got the blisters, sunburn, and body odor to prove it. We hiked the Zion Narrows, a five-mile long trek through a rocky stream with hundred-foot cliffs right above us. We rode horses around the spectacular red, orange, and white hoodoos of Bryce Canyon, and finished with two days of hiking and gazing at hundreds of natural sandstone arches in, you guessed it, Arches. Utah is simply a natural wonder.

But today the real fun begins. We're heading home. And when I say home, I mean we're driving back to Vegas. It may not be home to everyone in the Oakley family (Claire, I'm looking at you), but it's home to me. I just absolutely love the place. There are so many reasons for my love affair with Las Vegas: The hookers. The blow. The free liquor. Cirque du Soleil. The huevos rancheros at the Bellagio. Celine Dion. Three-card-poker at O'Sheas. Blackjack at the El Cortez. The neon. OK, just kidding about Cirque du Soleil. I hate Cirque de Soleil. Especially the O Show.

Seriously, the reason I love Vegas so much is simple: It's the ultimate escape for me. It's the one place I have absolutely no responsibility for anyone except for myself. No clients. No employees. No plans. No expectations. And best of all, no wife and no kids. Oh, wait a minute . . . I brought them with me this time.

The Oakley family arrived at Caesars Palace around five in the afternoon. We checked in and got two rooms on the eighteenth floor. It was fantastic to finally have a hot shower, and even better to have a few minutes away from the kids. We both showered off the trail dust, hung out for an hour or so, and decided it was time for a cocktail and dinner. We texted the kids and went to a bar near the Caesars Sports Book.

The four of us sat down, and the waiter asked us what we would like to drink. I ordered a Budweiser. Claire requested a Tito's and soda with slices of orange and lime. Sydney ordered the same. Lucas ordered a Blue Moon. Claire's mouth dropped wide open. She was aware that Lucas had a fake ID he used at college bars, but she had never seen him use it. The waiter asked Sydney and Lucas for their IDs. He looked at Sydney's first and handed it back to her. Lucas handed his ID to him and he examined it closely. He scrutinized the front and the back, then looked up at Lucas and said, "I'll be back in a minute," and walked away with his license.

"OK, that's weird," I said.

"Dad, he knows it's a fake," Sydney said emphatically. "I've seen this happen in Chapel Hill."

"What's your birthday on that ID, Lucas?"

"September 16, 1994. It's my birthday, just two years earlier. So, I'm 21."

"Using a false ID is a felony in Las Vegas. Lucas could get arrested. Or we could get arrested as parents. I think we should leave," Claire said.

"Leave?" I said.

"I think it's a good idea. Lucas, you should leave," Sydney said. "I'd leave if it were me."

"C'mon Lucas, let's go," Claire said. She grabbed her purse and made a beeline out of the bar and into the casino. Lucas followed close behind.

Sydney and I stayed there and waited for our drinks. It was taking forever. The bar was not crowded at all. Maybe five other people were there. Finally, a different waiter brought three drinks to our table. Nothing for Lucas, and no sign of the waiter who took his license.

Syd took a sip of her drink and said, "I don't feel comfortable here. I'm going to go find them."

"OK," I said, "I'll text you when I finish my beer and we can meet up."

I sat there sipping my Bud for what seemed like an hour, but it was more like ten minutes. The waiter walked back up, holding Lucas's license.

"Where'd everyone go?"

"Mesa Grille texted us and said our table was ready. They left for dinner. The only reason I'm here is that you have my son's ID."

"I see," he said.

"Could I settle up?"

"This ID that your son gave me is a fake."

"Oh really?" I said. "I don't know whether it's fake or not. I do know one thing though. I know how old my son is. He's twenty-one. He was born on September 16, 1994. He turned twenty-one last fall."

"Well, I don't know how old he is. Because this is a fake ID. Normally when a kid gives me a fake, I keep it and call Caesars security. But since you're his dad and vouched for him, I'm going to give it back to you."

"Well, thanks so much," I said with not a little dose of sarcasm. He handed me back the license.

"One more thing: Your son is not welcome in this bar. And for that matter, neither are you."

"Don't worry, I won't be back."

I stood up, chugged the rest of my Bud, breathed a huge sigh of relief, and walked out and back into the casino. When I got out of sight of the bar, I texted to find out where everyone was. They were on the other side of the Forum Shoppes, which is about a half mile away. They told me to meet them in front of Joe's Stone Crab, a nearby seafood restaurant.

When I got there, Lucas looked different.

"Is that what you were wearing before?"

"No, I took my sweatshirt off so they wouldn't recognize me."

"That was my idea," Claire said. "Jesus, I thought we were going to spend the night in jail."

"We weren't going to spend the night in jail," I said, already sensing that the assault was just beginning.

"What are you talking about? Lucas could have been arrested and we could have too. What kind of parents are we? The kind that encourages our kids to lie about who they are?"

"I didn't tell Lucas it was OK to order a beer. He just ordered it on his own. Let's not make this into a bigger deal than it is," I said. "Besides, when we were eighteen, it was legal to have a beer."

"But it's not legal now. And we're showing our kids that it's fine to flat-out lie about who they are."

For the next hour, we had a nice quiet dinner. Except for the nice part. It was quiet. There just wasn't much to more to say. We were all tired from hiking all week and our first two hours of relaxing in Vegas had turned into a total scene. After our meal was done, I quickly paid the check and we went back to our rooms.

Claire and I both agreed that we would not be coming back to Vegas with the kids until they were both twenty-one. This was way too much stress. We switched on the TV for a few minutes, and then I told Claire that I could watch TV in Charlotte, and I was going to go downstairs and play some blackjack. Normally she wouldn't be happy about that, but that night I think she was happy that the child corrupter was getting out of her sight.

I walked down the hall to Lucas and Sydney's room. They were watching TV. I told them that I was going to the Cromwell to play blackjack and that if Sydney wanted to play, that's where I'd be.

Fast-forward to two hours later. I'm playing craps at the Cromwell. Someone hits me on the elbow. I turn around and it's Sydney and Lucas. I was psyched to see them, especially since I wasn't doing that well at craps.

"Dad, you wanna play some blackjack?" Sydney asked.

"Sure," I said. I gathered my chips from the craps table, and we found an open blackjack table just a few feet away.

"Syd and I are going to play. Lucas, what are you going to do?"

"I'll walk around and watch you guys."

Sydney and I sat down at the blackjack table. We were the only two people playing. Syd put $60 on the table and showed her ID. I bought in for $200.

Syd knew how to play blackjack but had never played in a casino. Her first hand was a pair of eights. She knew from all the home games we'd played over the years that you always split eights and aces. She won both hands and never looked back. She started on a hot streak and didn't cool down.

It was pretty cool to be playing cards in Vegas with my daughter. It seemed like only yesterday that she was an infant, and now she was my blackjack buddy. I thought, *I can't wait for Lucas to be old enough to play.*

At that instant, Lucas walked up to the other end of the table. He put $100 on the table and brazenly handed his ID to the dealer. Yes, it was the very same ID he had used at the bar four hours earlier. The dealer eyeballed it for about two seconds and said, "Welcome to the table. Would you like green or red chips?"

"Red," Lucas said.

Lucas looked across the table and said, "How ya doing, family?"

I was in a state of total disbelief. What a pair of balls this kid had. Before I could say anything—and what would I say anyway?—the dealer dealt our cards, and suddenly we were all playing blackjack. We all won our first hand together.

Then the cocktail waitress stopped by, and Lucas asked for a Tito's and soda. I almost fell off my chair. I recovered in time to order a Bud, and Syd ordered a Bud Light. The next few hours were a total blur. The next time I looked at my watch it was four in the morning. When I realized how late it was, we cashed in our chips. We had each won over $200.

We headed back across Las Vegas Boulevard to Caesars Palace. When we got to the statue of Caesar in the lobby, I made them set the alarms on their phones. We had to get up to go to the Neon Museum Tour at 9:00 a.m.

Lucas and Sydney three hours before they had to wake up to go to the Neon Museum.

When my alarm went off, a mere three hours later, I felt like most people do after a night in Vegas. Like shit. But I had to rally. And more importantly, I had to make sure the kids rallied. I texted them. No reply. I called them. No answer. Finally, I decided to walk down the hall to their room and knock on the door. No answer. I kept banging until the door finally opened—the door behind me across the hall. I apologized to man I woke up and kept knocking. Then the door of the room beside them opened. I apologized to another guy. Finally, Lucas came to their door. He looked almost as good as I felt.

"C'mon guys, we gotta go. We have to leave for the Neon Museum in ten minutes."

"Do we have to go?" Lucas whined.

"Yes, a deal is a deal," I said. I walked past Lucas into their room, "Wake up, Syd. Mom's ready to go."

Miraculously, both of them were dressed and ready to leave in five minutes. The three of us quickly walked back to our room to get Claire. Totally unaware of what had transpired four hours earlier, she looked at Lucas and said sarcastically, "Lucas, don't forget your ID."

"Oh, I never leave home without it."

THE MIDDLE SEAT

When you're traveling with your family, no matter where you are, no matter how great the place you're in, after a certain amount of time, your kids will get on your nerves. It's a fact. We've traveled all over the place with Syd and Lucas, and as cool as they are, sometimes they can be annoying. OK, well not sometimes. Every time.

It's just a matter of when the annoyance will start.

I think there are probably different annoyance time limits for different destinations. For instance, if the four of us are driving together to my mom's house in Creedmoor, the nerve-getting-on can commence as quickly as ten seconds into the drive. Literally as we are backing down the driveway. Usually it has to do with Sydney not getting her shit packed in time, or Lucas forgetting his headphones, both of which make us late. Not that any of us really want to get to Creedmoor early, but that's not the point. It just proves that sometimes the nerve-getting-on starts before we begin our trip.

Sometimes we don't get on each other's nerves for a couple of days. New York trips are like this. There's so much for everyone to do there, we can do our own things. Usually the trouble starts when something simple happens, like when Lucas asked Claire to put his Tom Ford sunglasses in her purse at a bar, and somehow the next day they were nowhere to be found. Lucas got annoyed with Claire that she lost them, and Claire got annoyed with Lucas, because she told him it was getting dark in twenty minutes and that he should leave his sunglasses in the hotel room.

I'm sure Sydney and Lucas get annoyed with us sometimes too. We constantly remind them how lucky they are. They are lucky. Claire and I are really cool parents, and we have taken them on some amazing trips over the years: Jackson Hole, Paris, Berlin, Vegas, Breckenridge, San Francisco, and of course—Creedmoor. OK, we never took them to Disney World. We just don't like theme parks. And we hate Disney. In all honesty, we did take them to Disneyland for a half day when they were in elementary school, when we were on a TV shoot in California, just to have something to talk about with some of the other parents in South Charlotte. But that's beside the point.

We think Sydney and Lucas won the parent lottery. Here's proof: We just took them to Hawaii.

Today we are finishing a fourteen-day trip to Oahu and Kauai. Our friend G.W. Mix runs the Hawaii Bowl and invited us to join his family in Honolulu for the game. The four of us stayed at the iconic Sheraton Waikiki—iconic because it's the hotel where the Brady Bunch stayed on their visit. We stayed there for eight days, and then we traveled to Kauai, the Garden Isle. This is where Claire and I went on our honeymoon thirty years ago. When we came home after our honeymoon, we swore we would come back to Kauai every year. Ah, naïve honeymooner dreams. This is the first year we returned, and it was extra special to return with our children.

The Kauai trip has been relatively annoyance free. In fact, I think being in paradise has helped us set the record for the least amount of kid induced annoyances ever on a trip. Unless you count Lucas walking super-fast on hikes and leaving us behind with no water or provisions (he had the backpack) because he wanted to get back to the hotel to watch the latest episode of *My 600-Lb Life*. Or Sydney suddenly deciding that she needed to take a shower ten minutes before we were supposed to be at the Hawaii Bowl banquet. These are minor annoyances, and in my opinion, don't really count. Until we got to the airport today for the return trip home, we were on a record-setting thirteen-day non-annoyance streak.

At the Kauai airport we checked in at the American counter. Claire and Sydney were on the same reservation. Lucas and I were each on our own reservations because we had booked at different times—Lucas was flying for free on frequent-flier miles. Claire and Sydney checked in first and I could tell that something was not quite right. Sydney was in a window seat, 12A, and Claire was a couple of rows behind her in a middle seat, 14B. Claire isn't normally one to complain about her seat on a plane, but our flight to Los Angeles was six hours long. The American employee told Claire that the flight was full, and that she could talk with the agent at the gate about getting a window seat, but not to get her hopes up. Claire said that was fine, but I knew that it really wasn't fine. Claire was annoyed. I was really hoping that it would get worked out at the gate. I checked in next and I was assigned a window seat, 15F. Lucas checked in, and he was assigned a window seat too, 14A.

Claire asked Lucas and me where our seats were, and when we told her, she was pissed. "How can I be Advantage Gold and get put in a middle seat on a six-hour flight?" It was a good question, especially considering where Lucas was sitting.

As we were waiting to go through security, Claire was fuming. I started thinking it through, and it was a bit odd that Claire was in a middle seat. Claire and Sydney were booked on the same itinerary. There's no way those two booked Claire in a random middle seat. *Wait a minute*, I thought. I turned and asked Lucas again, "What seat are you in?"

"14A," he said.

A couple of minutes later I said to Claire, "What seat are you in again?"

"14B, a middle seat!"

"I know," I said and didn't say anything else. But I realized that Lucas was sitting beside her. *That's very odd*, I thought.

When Claire went to the bathroom, I said to the kids, "One of you should offer to switch seats with your mom."

"I really want a window seat," Lucas said.

"So do I, Dad," Sydney said, "I don't like to be between strangers on a flight."

"You wouldn't be between strangers if you sat in the middle and let Mom sit by the window. I don't care which one of you does it, but one of you will be giving up your window seat to your mom."

"What about you, Dad? You could give Mom your window seat and sit in the middle beside me."

That's the moment the annoyance started for me, a full thirty minutes after it started with Claire. "Are you serious, Lucas? You will give your mom your window seat. And that's that."

About the time Claire got back from the bathroom, it hit me: Sydney and Lucas must have gone on to the American Airlines app and switched their seats around. That would explain how Lucas had magically been seated next to Claire, and Sydney had gotten her own window seat. I thought about it a couple more minutes and decided that was definitely what had happened. I could just see those two brats sitting together giggling at how they were going to pull one over on their mom.

Claire made one last-ditch effort to get her own window seat at the gate, but the agent told her that the plane was entirely full and that her middle seat was the only seat they had available. Soon thereafter the gate agent called Group 4, and we lined up to board. Sydney was the first Oakley to hand her ticket to be scanned. The gate agent said, "Oh, Sydney Oakley, are you traveling with David Oakley?"

"Yes," Sydney said, and looked at me.

"That's me," I said.

"Your upgrade to first class has come through, Mr. Oakley."

"Really?" I said. A smile came across my face, thinking about how nice it was going to be to stretch out, have a cocktail or three, and relax in first class . . . This fantasy lasted for all of two seconds when I realized that I would be divorced when I landed if the following words didn't come out of my mouth immediately: "Could my wife take my first-class ticket?"

"Sure," the gate agent said. "Will you stand over here while I reticket you?" She then scanned Lucas's ticket, and he followed Sydney down the jetway to the plane. "Is your wife's name Claire?"

"Yes," I said, thinking that she was putting her in my seat. "Well, it looks like we have two seats in first class, and both of you are getting upgraded."

"What, are you serious?" Claire exclaimed. "This is the nicest thing ever. Wow!"

They reticketed us, in 5A and 5F, both window seats.

"This is so cool," I said, thrilled that we were in first class. Our day was definitely turning around.

"Maybe we could ask someone to change seats so we could sit together?" Claire said.

"But then we one of us would have to sit on the aisle,"

"I really want a window seat," Claire said.

"So do I," I said.

"I guess we'll have to sit across from each other," she said.

"That's cool with me."

We walked into the plane and back to row 5. There was a friendly guy and his young son sitting in the aisle seats of our row. He looked up at us and said, "Are you guys traveling together?"

"Yes,"

"In both of these window seats?"

"Yes."

"Would you like to sit together? That way my son and I could sit together," he said with a genuine look of affection for his son.

"Sure," I said with a grin, "but only if she lets me have the window seat."

Claire magically dropped her demand for her window seat as soon as the father said he wanted to sit with his son. But it wasn't maternal instinct that swayed Claire. It was the fact that the guy was Anthony Kiedis, the lead singer for the Red Hot Chili Peppers. And Claire would get to sit across the aisle from him for the next six hours.

Sydney and Lucas might have won the parent lottery. But Claire got upgraded.

YOU'LL FIGURE IT OUT

Not long after I graduated from UNC, my dad and I went to lunch at Shoney's in Durham. It was one of my dad's favorite spots. We had eaten there many times over the years, but I'll never forget this meal. I was twenty-two years old and had no idea what I wanted to do next. Actually, what I really wanted was go party for another four years in Chapel Hill, but that wasn't an option.

What was an option was getting a job working in the family business, Cedar Creek Pottery, as sales manager of the craft gallery. It was a good job, and it paid pretty well, but my heart wasn't in it.

The waitress brought us each a slice of strawberry pie. My dad took a bite and asked, "So what do you want to do?"

"I don't know."

"You don't know?"

"I don't know what I want to do," I looked past my dad and stared outside down Roxboro Road. "Look out there," I said. "Look at all those signs."

Sid turned and looked too.

"See that Exxon sign there? Every time I see an Exxon sign, I wonder why they changed the name from Esso to Exxon, and I wonder why the name Exxon is in red and why there is a blue rectangle under it. Why couldn't the type be green and the rectangle be yellow? Or why does the *M* for McDonald's have to be gold? Why couldn't it have been purple instead? Who makes those decisions?"

He didn't answer; he just looked at me with an expression that said, *Who the hell is sitting across from me and what kind of drugs is he on?*

"I just see myself doing something with outdoor signs and logos."

"Well, just do it," he said.

I mean my dad was cool, but I didn't realize that he was so hip to the groove that he knew Nike's tagline before it was even written, but I swear to God he said Just Do It.

"I want to do it," I said. "I just don't know *how* to do it."

"You'll figure it out. You've got time."

"What do you mean I've got time? I've got to get a job. I just graduated."

"You've got plenty of time, Dave. I have a lot of friends who are in their forties and they don't know what the fuck they're going do with their lives. They're twice your age. Think about that for a minute. People twice your age don't know what they're going to do with their lives. So according to that, you've got plenty of time to decide. Take a little pressure off yourself and you'll figure it out."

It was one of the best pieces of advice I've ever gotten. I eventually figured out how to get into advertising, and it became my passion. I'll never forget how important that conversation with my dad was in determining my direction in life.

Now, thirty years later, my son Lucas is a twenty-two-year-old graduate of the University of North Carolina at Chapel Hill. He and I had lunch recently, and he is trying to figure out his career direction. He's interested in fashion and streetwear brands, but he thinks he should consider graphic design to start. He told me that's he's not sure what he wants to do. I told him about my conversation with my dad when I was his age and what my father said to me.

When I finished telling him about our talk at Shoney's, Lucas smiled and said, "So, you're telling me to relax and I'll figure it out?"

"No, that's what your grandfather would have told you," I said. "I'm telling you to get a fucking job."

Which dad gave the better advice? Only time will tell.

PART IV

THEY'RE JUST PEOPLE . . .

"They're just people," Claire always reminds me when we're around celebrities. Not that it happens all that often, but being in the ad business, every once in a while, the planets align, and we find ourselves in the presence of a well-known person. "It's important to just act naturally and not gawk at them," she tells me every single time. The two of us have had our share of celebrity encounters: Bruce Springsteen, Chris Rock, Michael Jordan, Ric Flair, Steven Tyler, Cindy Lauper, Tom Carlin, Lauren Hutton, Sigourney Weaver, Steve Townley, Anthony Kiedis, Rodney Dangerfield, and many more. Claire always remains cool as a cucumber in their presence. Except for one time when we sat down for dinner in Los Angeles, one of the greatest musicians of all time was escorted in and sat down at a table right across from us. It was Stevie Wonder. Claire would not stop looking at him. She was a huge fan and had all his albums, but her staring was even making me uncomfortable. She finally took her eyes off him and looked across the table at me. "What?" she said. "It's not like he can see me."

MEETING MALCOLM GLADWELL

I love doing TV production in Los Angeles. You work with the most talented directors and crew in the world. You get to stay at swanky oceanfront hotels like Shutters on the Beach. You eat at the finest restaurants, and your client pays for it all. But what I love the most about shooting in Hollywood is you never know when you'll run into a celebrity. When you do, you have to remember not to get starstruck. They're just regular people, and in LA they do things that regular people do. Like go out to dinner. So, it just stands to reason that sometimes you run into famous folks when you eat out.

Last night was one of those nights. We were in Santa Monica enjoying a preshoot meal at the Rustic Canyon restaurant with our Bojangles' clients. I was sitting at a large table between Randy Poindexter and Mike Bearss and across from Grant Springer, Eric Roch von Rochsburg, Laura George, and Claire. We were talking about how excited we were about the commercials we were shooting the next day. They weren't typical ads. They were edgy concepts—the type that people would notice and talk about—and hopefully would motivate people to buy some Bojangles' biscuits.

As Mike topped off my wine glass, I noticed a familiar face behind Laura. Right outside on the patio enjoying dinner was none other than Malcolm Gladwell, the author. I leaned over to Mike and said, "Look at that table outside—it's Malcolm Gladwell."

"Where?"

"Behind Laura," I said as I motioned toward the window. "That's him, right?"

"Look him up," Mike said.

So I googled Malcolm Gladwell on my phone. I pulled up a couple of images of him and showed Mike.

"Yeah, that's him," he confirmed.

"I can't believe it, this is so cool," I said. "He's had such a big influence on me over the years. Have you read any of his work?" I asked Mike.

"Yeah, *Tipping Point* and *Outliers* and . . . another one, I can't think of the name right now."

"You should read *Purple Cow*. The whole premise is that you have to do something really different to stand out and be noticed. When you're driving down the highway and pass a field of black-and-white cows you just think, *That's a field of cows*, and keep driving. But what if one of those cows was purple? You'd probably stop your car, get out and take pictures of that purple cow because you've never seen anything like that before. It's a simple and brilliant premise. And the core of what I believe in as a guy who creates advertising for a living."

"Sounds cool," Mike said, "I'll have to order a copy."

The meal was one of the best I had ever had. And even though the conversation was easy and fun, I was a bit preoccupied. I kept glancing beyond Laura to the table outside to make sure Malcolm was still there. He was sitting with a couple of friends and was about halfway through dinner. Then he looked at his watch, stood up, and walked over to the valet stand. *Oh shit*, I thought, *he's leaving.*

"I'll be right back," I said to my table, and I got up and walked outside.

I walked up behind Malcolm at the valet stand and tapped him on the right shoulder, and quickly stood on his left. He turned to his right and no one was there and then looked back to his left and saw me there.

"Are you Malcolm?" I asked.

"Yes," he said with a shy smile.

"Hi, I'm David Oakley, and I just wanted to come out and tell you how much I've enjoyed reading your books and what a big influence you've had on my career."

"Well, thanks, that's very nice of you to say."

"I really liked *Tipping Point* and *Outliers*, but my favorite by far was *Purple Cow*. By far."

"Oh . . ." Malcolm nodded.

"A few years ago, we did a billboard for Bloom Supermarkets where we had a giant muffin fall off the billboard and crush a car. It got a lot of attention and somehow you heard about it and contacted our client, the marketing director at Bloom, and told her that that billboard was a perfect example of a Purple Cow. She was thrilled, and I must say it was one of the highlights of my career. Thank you for doing that. That was so cool of you to take the time to do that."

Malcolm just nodded again, looking anxiously at the valet guy who had just driven up with his car.

"I know you're leaving, but would you mind if I took a photo with you?"

"OK," he said.

I pulled out my iPhone and snapped a quick selfie.

"Thank you so much, Malcolm. Meeting you has made my night."

I walked back into the restaurant and sat back down to finish dinner with the biggest smile on my face. I showed everyone the photo of Malcolm and me.

"I can't believe you went and talked with him, Oakley. That's pretty awesome," Randy said.

"Oh, he's just a person," I said. "I'm sure he appreciates knowing how his work has had such an impact on me."

Malcolm Gladwell and his biggest fan.

The next morning as I was driving through the California countryside to our shoot location, I was thinking how lucky I was to have met Malcolm Gladwell the night before. I smiled as we passed a field of cows. I looked hard, but there wasn't a single purple cow there. Then I was struck with a horrifying realization. I gasped, and the smile quickly vanished from my face. "Oh my God, I'm a fucking idiot. Malcolm Gladwell didn't write Purple Cow. Seth Godin wrote Purple Cow." I started laughing at myself and couldn't stop for miles.

Malcolm Gladwell must have thought that I'd lost my mind. No wonder he barely said anything to me. I'd just thought he was humble and shy. I'm sure as he drove away, he laughed about it and thought of me as . . . an Outlier.

Maybe. But more probably, he saw me for what I was: a jackass.

A purple jackass.

AUTOGRAPH

I was sitting at the kitchen table yesterday with my teenaged niece and nephew, Emily and Carson. They're in town staying with us for Thanksgiving.

"Do you guys ever make crank calls?" I asked them. "I loved doing that when I was your age."

They both gave me a look that clearly indicated they had no idea what I was talking about. Claire, who was at the sink washing the coffee pot, heard the question and laughed out loud. "You can't make crank calls anymore, David."

"What are you talking about?"

"Caller ID. Duh!"

"Huh?" I said, not understanding.

"You can't crank call anymore because phones have caller ID," Claire said in her super slow methodical voice that she uses when she tries to explain something to a total idiot. "They can see who's calling."

"Ohhhh," I said, finally getting it. "I never thought about that. Well, that sucks,"

"Who would you crank call?" Emily asked.

"Random people," I said.

"Give us an example," she prodded.

"The standard crank call was when you call a number and someone would answer, you would ask if their refrigerator was running. And when they responded yes, I would say 'Well, you better catch it before it gets away!'"

I looked around to catch their appreciative smiles. But I got none.

Carson, stone-faced, asked, "And you thought that was funny?"

"I said that was the standard one. I think my favorite one was when we would call the Days Inn Motel on Redwood Road. When the front desk answered I would say, 'Hi, this is Mr. Duke from Room 317. Umm . . . this is a little embarrassing . . . but I'm in the bathroom and well, I had an upset stomach and there's no toilet paper in here. Do you think you could bring some up here?' Every time they would say something like, 'Oh I'm so sorry, Mr. Duke, I'll bring some right up.' That was probably my favorite."

Emily grinned slightly and looked at her brother. I sighed, thinking how these youngsters had no idea what they had missed. Caller ID has ruined one of my greatest pleasures of my teenage years. But that's not the only thing that technology has killed.

"Emily," I asked, "if you ran into a famous athlete or singer in a restaurant, would you ask them for an autograph?"

"No, I'd probably just sneak a picture of them. Or ask them to take a selfie with me."

"Right. The selfie has killed autograph collecting."

I've always liked autograph collecting, even though it's always been kind of an odd hobby. What does someone signing their name on a piece of paper really mean? And why is it so cherished? It's just some scribble on a card. Does it prove that you've had an encounter with this notable person?

Nevertheless, this didn't prevent me from being an obsessive autograph collector when I was a teenager. But I didn't stalk famous people in person. I wrote them letters.

It all started when one day when I read an article in the *Durham Morning Herald*. The newspaper story said that people were writing threatening letters to Hank Aaron. They were calling him names, telling him they hated him, and if he broke Babe Ruth's home run record, they would kill him. Well, that seemed a little over the top.

Hank wasn't my favorite baseball player, not even close. He didn't play for my favorite team, the Cincinnati Reds. He played for the Atlanta Braves. I hated the Braves. I didn't hate them enough that I wanted to kill their players if they somehow beat the Reds, but I still hated them.

I decided that Hank might need a little support. I wanted him to know that not every white guy in the South was rooting against him in his quest to be the all-time home-run king.

So on a lined sheet of notebook paper, I hand-wrote a letter of encouragement to Hank. I told him that he was my favorite player and that I was a big fan of the Atlanta Braves. I told him that I was his number-one fan. God, I was such a liar.

I also wrote that I was rooting for him to break Babe Ruth's record. That part was true. I wanted him to be the all-time home-run king. I finished the letter by asking him if he would send me his autograph. I even included a stamped self-addressed envelope. I addressed the envelope to Hank Aaron c/o the Atlanta Braves, Fulton County Stadium, Atlanta, Georgia.

About a month later, I got a letter in the mail. It was an odd-looking envelope, and I couldn't figure out why until I realized that it was because my name and address were in my own handwriting. *It's the envelope I sent to Hammering Hank!* I quickly tore open the envelope; inside was a color photo of Hank Aaron, signed, *To David, Best Wishes, Hank Aaron.* I couldn't believe it. Hank Aaron had read my letter and sent me an autograph.

By the time the mailman came to pick up our outgoing mail the next day, I had written letters to Johnny Bench, Pete Rose, Joe Morgan, and ten other assorted baseball and football players.

This was the start of an obsession.

Over the next year or so, I wrote hundreds of letters to athletes.

My first autograph: Home-run king Hank Aaron.

More often than not, I'd get a response. Brooks Robinson from the Orioles sent an autographed picture and Orioles stickers within a week. So I wrote him again. And he sent me another autograph. And more stickers. By the end of that summer, I had eleven Brooks Robinson autographs.

Richard Petty had the most ornate signature. Roger Staubach's was probably my favorite. Dean Smith actually typed me a letter thanking me for being such a big Tar Heel fan. I put them all into a special album that I cleverly titled *Autographs*. I still have it today, and it's one of my most cherished possessions.

I never really thought that maybe the autographs weren't from the actual sports figures. That maybe someone else had signed them. Maybe these ballplayers got so many letters that they hired an assistant or someone from their family to sign autographs for them.

That thought never crossed my mind until I was in my early twenties at a Baltimore Orioles game. I was with my cousin Ken, and we had driven to Baltimore to see the Orioles play the Kansas City Royals.

During the game, we consumed way more than our share of National Bohemians, and as soon as it was over, we thought it would be a good idea to go down to the locker room entrance to get an autograph or two from some Oriole players. When we got there, the place was mobbed with kids waiting to do the same. Kids between six and twelve years old. Ken and I felt a little out of place. Especially when one of the kids asked us what we were doing there.

"We're waiting for some of our friends on the Orioles to come out," I said.

"You guys know some of the Orioles?" a kid asked.

"Yeah, we know a lot of them," I nodded.

Then the boy whispered something to his friend and the friend looked at us and said, "Do you play baseball?"

"Yeah, but we don't play for the Orioles."

"Who do you play for?"

"Kansas City," I quickly said.

"Oh. Can I get your autograph?"

I winked at Ken, and he just looked at me and shook his head.

"Sure," I said, "Hand me your glove. You got a Sharpie?"

The kid handed me his Wilson glove. I quickly scribbled my signature. Truthfully, it wasn't my signature. Since I couldn't remember the name of anyone who played for Kansas City, I quickly scribbled the first name I could think of that wasn't David Oakley.

Ronald Reagan, of course.

"Thanks," the kid said, beaming up at me.

"You're welcome," I said. "You should get his autograph too," I said and pointed to Ken. I watched as Ken signed *Mick Jagger* on the same glove. His friend then handed me his glove. I signed his *George Washington*. At least that sounds like a baseball player.

In the next ten minutes we must have signed twenty caps, programs, and gloves. Word to the wise: If you ever see a Baltimore Orioles cap on eBay that's autographed by Farrah Fawcett, rest assured it's a fake. But if it's not too much money, please buy it for me.

BECAUSE I SAID I WOULD

One of the things I love about working in advertising is that I meet so many interesting, innovative, and inspiring people.

Of course, I actually meet a lot of insensitive, intolerant, and insecure people, too. Usually they make for better stories.

But I met someone last week who was the exception. His name is Alex Sheen, and he started a social movement called Because I said I would.

I was in Destin, Florida, with Claire, Sarah Peter, and Laura Wallace—colleagues from my office. We were there to present our new brand advertising campaign for Destin-Fort Walton Beach at the Okaloosa County annual meeting.

After a forty-five-minute presentation where we showed all our new work for 2020, Jennifer Adams, our client, introduced the keynote speaker for the event: Alex Sheen. I really didn't know that much about Alex, but I listened intently as he told his story. He talked about his father and what a great influence he had been on him. His dad wasn't anything out of the ordinary—in Alex's words, "a nerdy pharmacist." But one day his dad got a call from the hospital, and the doctor told him that he had stage-four lung cancer. He had less than six months to live. Of course, this was a shock to everyone, but Alex's father decided to tackle the cancer the most aggressive way possible. He did chemo and radiation, and six months later, he was cancer free. They celebrated together, but the celebration didn't last that long. The cancer soon came back, and Alex's father passed away about a year later.

Alex was asked to give the eulogy at his father's funeral. He was overcome with grief and didn't know what he was going to say. He kept thinking about his dad, and what stood out to him was that he had always been there for him. His dad always came to his soccer games. He always came home for dinner. He did what he said he was going to do. He was committed to his family. But now he had been taken away. It wasn't fair. He was too young. How was Alex going to go on without him?

Alex said, "My father was an average man. He didn't run marathons, he didn't write books, he wasn't a war hero. He was average. An everyday person. Almost unnoticeable. Except . . . for one thing: My father was a man of his word. He was there when I needed him." Alex titled his father's eulogy "Because I said I would."

At the funeral, Alex talked about the importance of a promise, and for the first time, he handed out what he called "Promise Cards." It was a simple idea, a blank business card with five words written at the bottom: *Because I said I would.* He asked the congregation to write a promise on the card and give it to someone as a symbol of their commitment. The Promise Card helps hold you accountable for your commitment. An example is, *I promise not to text and drive. Because I said I would.*

The Promise Card was so well received by those in attendance at his father's funeral that he decided to post the idea online. Alex offered to send ten Promise Cards to anyone anywhere in the world at no cost to them.

"I would get three or four emails a day asking me for cards," he said. "It was pretty cool."

Then one morning, it all changed.

He woke and checked his email and there were fifteen thousand emails in his inbox. He thought there must be some kind of mistake, but then he noticed that Mashable had written a story about the

Promise Cards. The story then got picked up internationally, and the next morning he had thirty thousand requests.

His message had gone viral.

"OK," Alex said to the audience in Destin, "it's one thing to send out three or four packs of Promise Cards every day, but thirty thousand? Do you know how much that is in postage? $15,000. I don't know about you, but I didn't just have that kind of money lying around to spend on stamps," he said, then laughed. I thought, *I've got $10,000 in my closet, but I wouldn't spend it on stamps either.*

But Alex had made a commitment. The importance of a promise resonated around the world. Promise made. Promise kept. Commitment. So he somehow found a way to fund the stamps.

Alex continued his speech, giving examples of some of the promise cards that people sent to him. *I will lose weight. I will donate a kidney to my brother. I will sincerely complement one person every day.*

He told the story of another father in Richmond, Virginia, who was told he had six months to live. This father had been putting "napkin notes" of encouragement in his daughter's lunch box since she was in first grade. His daughter was in the eighth grade then. He filled out a promise card that said, *My daughter will receive a napkin note every day until she graduates from high school.* He passed away four months later, but not before he wrote 1600 napkin notes. His daughter got one every day until she got her diploma. He was true to his word.

Since his father's funeral in 2012, Alex has distributed over 3.15 million Promise Cards to over 220 countries around the world. By request only.

It was one of the most moving and cool stories I had ever heard. People from all over the globe were filling out his cards and making commitments to others. Just like his dad did to him. It was truly inspiring.

At the end of his presentation, Alex gave ten blank *Because I said I would* cards to everyone in attendance. I took mine and put them in my back pocket.

A few hours later, we were at the airport walking to our gate, and I saw Alex waiting for his plane. He was wearing headphones sitting at a table, playing a video game on his computer. He didn't see us as we walked by. I said to Sarah, Claire, and Laura, "I need to write something on one of his cards and give it to him."

I thought about it for a minute, grinned, grabbed a pen and scribbled a promise on a *Because I said I would* card.

I handed the card to them. The three of them all busted out laughing.

"You can't do that, though," Claire said.

"It's funny, but he's really serious about his cause," Sarah said.

"Yes, he is, and it's a great cause, but he does have a sense of humor," I said.

"Not about that," Sarah said. "I'll give you $50 bucks if you walk up to him and give him that card."

"Really?" I said.

"Yeah, I'll give you $50."

"You're not really going to give that him," Laura said. "He won't think it's funny."

"We'll see. I could use $50. Thanks, Sarah."

I strolled back up the concourse to the Delta gate where Alex was sitting. Sarah positioned herself about twenty feet behind him, so she could verify whether I actually did it. I walked over to him and said, "Hi, Alex. I'm sorry to bother you, but I was at your presentation today, and well, I can't believe I'm running into you again so soon."

He stuck out his hand to shake mine and said, "Hello."

"I'm David Oakley, and I really enjoyed what you had to say. In fact, I filled out one of your cards and I want to give it to you."

"Oh, thank you, that's nice."

I reached into my back pocket and started fumbling around trying to find the card. I retrieved it and handed it to him.

The promise card read, *If I ever see Alex again, I'm going to kick his ass. Because I said I would.*

He looked at it and chuckled, "Wow," he said.

"Well, I guess now I'll have to fulfill my commitment. Because I said I would," I said. "Are you ready?"

He just looked at me. I paused for a moment and saw Sarah walking away. She knew she had to pay up.

Then I smiled. "I'm just kidding. My friend Sarah said she would give me $50 if I would walk up to you and give you this card."

He looked at the card again and said with a smile, "That's one of the strangest ones I've ever seen."

"Thanks for being a good sport. I'm going to give that $50 to your charity." I handed him two twenties and a ten. He laughed again and put the $50 in his backpack. He asked me to sit down, but I declined and said I had to catch my flight. He handed me his real business card and told me to keep spreading the word. And that's what I'm doing right now. Because I said I would.

Before I walked away, I asked him for one more thing. "Could I keep my Promise Card? And would you mind autographing it?"

"Sure," he chuckled.

He signed it, *Alex Sheen, worth the $50!*

I shook his hand again and wished him luck. I smiled as I walked back down the concourse toward the American Airlines gate, knowing that I had kept my promise to Sarah.

Too late, I realized that I should have taken a selfie with him. Autographs are so twentieth century.

AUNT HALLIE'S HEELS

Hollywood isn't the only place you can have a celebrity encounter. Our whole family had one recently in Chapel Hill. Claire, Sydney, Lucas, and I met my sister Lisa and her daughter Emily to see the Carolina Tar Heels play Florida State last Saturday. After the Tar Heels took care of business, we all walked from the Dean Dome to Franklin Street for some pizza and beer at IP3, the best pizza joint in town.

We found a table, put our jackets down, and got in line to order at the counter. That's when Claire whispered in my ear, "Look who's sitting at the table behind us."

I turned and saw a tall lanky fellow I recognized instantly: Tyler Hansbrough, the star of Carolina's 2009 national championship team. He was hanging out like a regular guy, having some pizza and beer.

Was I sure that it was him? Even sitting down, I could tell that this guy was really tall. Not to mention the fact that there were pictures of him all over the wall celebrating the Heels' championship win over Michigan State. If that weren't proof enough, even though he'd graduated a decade before, every five minutes someone would walk up and ask him to take a picture with them.

I took a swig of my Budweiser and asked my sixteen-year-old niece Emily, who is a huge Tar Heel basketball fan, if she knew why Tyler Hansbrough had decided to stay in school for his senior year at Carolina.

"No," she said.

"Everyone thinks he came back to win a national championship for North Carolina," I said.

"That's right," Lisa said, nodding.

"Or to atone for the ass-kicking that Kansas put on the Heels in the Final Four the year before," I said.

Lisa filled Emily in. "The Tar Heels fell behind by 40–12 to start that game. It was embarrassing."

"I didn't know that," Emily said.

"It certainly was no way for a great player to end his college basketball career," Lisa said.

"That's true," I said. "But the real reason Tyler played his senior season at Carolina is because of a chance meeting with our Aunt Hallie."

Aunt Hallie is now in her early eighties and has been a Carolina fan for as long as I can remember. She also is a big fan of her nieces and nephews, three of whom graduated from UNC. She hates Duke, but I'm not sure if that's because of the university, or because she was a nurse for forty years at Durham County General Hospital. Duke Hospital was their rival. Whatever the reason, she watches the Tar Heels whenever they're on TV. If they're winning, she'll stay up until midnight "to see my boys." But if they are having an off night, she'll walk up to the TV, turn it off, and say to herself, "If that's as good as you're going to play, I'm going to bed." I'm sure she was asleep by halftime the night of that Kansas game.

Aunt Hallie still lives in Butner and does most of her grocery shopping at the local Food Lion. But when she has a doctor's appointment, she shops at the Harris Teeter near University Mall in Chapel Hill. Why do I know this? Because one evening in the spring of 2008, a few weeks after the basketball season, Aunt Hallie called and told me about her trip to that Harris Teeter.

She said she was pushing her cart through the produce section

— 228 —

and noticing how their tomatoes weren't as red ripe as the ones she grew in her garden, when she looked up and saw a very tall man.

"This guy was the tallest person I had ever seen," she said to me, her voice full of excitement. "I knew he had to be a basketball player."

Aunt Hallie said she walked over to the man and looked up at him and said, "Do you play basketball?"

He looked down at Aunt Hallie, who is about five foot three, and said, "Yes, I do."

"I knew it, I knew it," she said and slapped her hands together for emphasis. "I knew you were a basketball player."

She paused for a second to look him straight in the eye. Then she asked, "Now tell me, do you play for Duke or for Carolina?"

"I play for Carolina," he patiently replied.

"Are you sure you don't play for Duke?"

"Uh, yeah, I'm sure."

"Well good, 'cause I wouldn't want to talk to you if you did."

Aunt Hallie said he looked at her like she was out of her mind. I'd imagine he was thinking something along the lines of *How could you not instantly recognize me? I just won the Naismith National Basketball Player of the Year Award.*

"What's your name?"

"Tyler. Tyler Hansbrough."

"You're Tyler?"

"Yes, I am."

"Well, Lord have mercy. I can't believe I'm standing here talking to Tyler. My name's Hallie."

"Nice to meet you, Hallie," he replied.

"I can't wait to tell my niece and nephews about who I met at the Harris Teeter. They went to Carolina too. You might know them. Do you know Lisa, Ken, and David Oakley?"

"No, I can't say that I do."

"Well, I guess you wouldn't know them. They graduated about twenty years ago."

She said she grabbed his hand and held it and said, "I can't believe I'm standing here in the Harris Teeter and I'm talking to Tyler." She said she squeezed his hand really tightly, patted it, and said, "Maybe next time I see you, I'll know who you are. And who you play for." She said she let out a loud laugh. She said Tyler smiled again and just kept looking at her with a puzzled look on his face like she was out of her frickin' mind.

Aunt Hallie called me and told me the whole story as soon as she got back to Butner. She didn't call me on the way home because she didn't have a cell phone in 2008. Or cable TV, for that matter. That's probably why she didn't recognize Tyler. The reception on her TV was like watching a basketball game through a Wisconsin blizzard.

The next day, there was a press conference at the Dean Dome. Hansbrough announced that he had decided to forgo the millions in NBA money to stay at Chapel Hill for his senior season. He said that he wanted to continue his college experience, and he wanted another chance to win the National Championship.

Tyler had some unfinished business to take care of. And it wasn't to cut down the nets in Detroit. No, I told Emily, Tyler Hansbrough stayed at Carolina for one reason: to prove to the sweet little lady at the Harris Teeter that he didn't play for Duke. And for that, fans of the 2009 NCAA Basketball Champion North Carolina Tar Heels owe a big batch of gratitude to our Aunt Hallie.

When I finished telling this story, Emily looked at me wide-eyed. "Is that true?"

"If you don't believe it, just ask him," I said.

We glanced over at his table and Emily grinned, then shook her head. She figured that if Tyler had already had a run-in with Aunt Hallie, he didn't need to be subjected to any more Oakley shenanigans. We let Tyler enjoy his piece of pizza in peace.

LOSING MY HEAD

The other night I was watching Ken Burns's amazing documentary *Country Music* on PBS. There was a segment featuring Dwight Yoakam and Buck Owens and their song, "Streets of Bakersfield." Burns talked about how this was the ultimate Nashville outsiders' song, and that Dwight and Buck debuted it together on the CMAs (Country Music Association Awards). Then they showed a clip of the two of them singing it together. It gave me goose bumps. *Oh, my goodness*, I thought, *I was there*. I'd been right on the side of the stage, watching them when they performed it live together that night, thirty-two years before.

I'll never, ever forget that evening. Not only because the performances were good. They were fantastic. And not only because I met some of country music's biggest stars. That night is forever etched in my memory because it was the night before I realized that my dad Sid was the worst fucking photographer in the history of the planet.

Can you tell I'm still mad about it?

It all started with a phone call in 1988. I was living in New York City at the time. Sid was on the line.

"Hey, David, you want to go to Nashville with me?"

"Nashville?"

"Yeah, a guy came into the shop today and gave me two tickets to see the CMA Awards in Nashville in October."

"Wait. What? A guy just walked into the shop and gave you two tickets? Are you shitting me, Sid?"

I started calling my dad Sid when I was thirteen and I started working in the family business along with college interns and apprentices who were seven to ten years older than me. They all called my dad Sid. At the time, I called him Daddy, but I wanted to be just one of the guys who worked for him, not his son who would get preferential treatment. At least that's what I thought at the time. So, I asked if I could call him Sid while I was working in the pottery shop. He said he was OK with it, and I called him Sid from that point on.

My dad was an extraordinarily talented artist, but his true gift was being able to talk with anyone about anything. He was a true conversationalist. He loved hearing people's stories.

His fans, as I called them, who came to his studio to buy his porcelain pots, would always ask him questions like "What temperature do you fire your work at?" or "How long have you been throwing pots? or, "What is it like to be an artist who actually makes a living doing what he loves?"

My dad would patiently answer the questions, but he would always turn the conversation back around to the person who was interested in his pottery.

"So, what do you do for a living?" my dad would ask.

"I'm an accountant. I've got a boring job," the customer would say, apologetically.

"Boring?" my dad would say. "I don't think it's boring to help people get an income tax refund. You probably bring joy to a lot of folks."

The guy would laugh and say, "It's not always refunds, though."

"Well, I guess that's true. Where do you do your work?"

"I'm from Shelby."

"Oh, I've been to Shelby. Do you ever eat at Bridges Barbeque?" For the next fifteen minutes, they wouldn't be talking about pottery or accounting; they would be talking about the best pork sandwich they had ever had.

Sometimes, when Sid really liked the person, he would give them a piece of his pottery. Now that I think about this, it may have been one of Sid's best sales techniques. Because usually after he gave someone a piece of his work, this person would buy a bunch more pottery. It's kind of like a drug dealer giving you a free crack sample. One hit and you're hooked. A customer for life.

That being said, I believe Sid sincerely had to like someone before he gave them a pot. Apparently, he must have really liked the guy from Nashville. Because on the phone that night, he told me he gave him a crystal vase that he'd made. This was the same kind of vase of his that was in the Smithsonian.

"David, I got to talking with him about the crystalline glaze on my pots and explained to him that the crystals form randomly during the firing. He was really interested, so I gave him one."

"Well, that was nice of you," I said as I stretched out on the couch.

"Then I asked him what he did for a living. He said he was a music producer in Nashville. So, I asked him what he produced his music on—a guitar, a banjo, or a mandolin?" Sid said.

"Do you know what a music producer is?" I said.

"I do now," he said. "Turns out he was the executive producer for the Country Music Association Awards Show in Nashville. Isn't that something?

"Wow, that's cool."

"He asked me if I liked country music. I said, 'Are you kidding me? I grew up on country music. I love it.' Then he asked me if I'd ever been to Nashville, and I said no, and he said how would you like to be my guest at this year's show? Can you believe that?"

"No. Did you believe him?"

"Not at first, but he gave me his business card. Billy Stratton, executive producer of the CMA Awards. So, David, do you want to go with me?"

"You know how much I love country music," I said. "Maybe Dwight will be there! This is going to be a crazy fun trip."

Two months later, I flew from New York to Nashville, took a cab from the airport, and met Sid at our hotel, the luxurious Days Inn off Interstate 40. He was waiting for me when the cab arrived, and as soon as he saw me, he said, "Put your bags in the room, let's go. We gotta get over to the Grand Ole Opry House now."

"But I thought the show was tomorrow night," I said.

"It is, but Billy called me at the shop yesterday and said we should come for the rehearsals today."

It didn't cross my mind that we might be eligible for any kind of VIP treatment. So I greeted this news with the same enthusiasm I would have had if he had asked me to watch a rerun of *Days of Our Lives.* "Aren't we going to see the same thing tomorrow night?"

"Yes, but let's go check it out." So off to the Grand Ole Opry House we went.

When we got there, Billy Stratton met us at the door. Sid introduced me to Billy and said, "David thought I had made up this whole story. He couldn't believe that I knew you."

"Well, it's true," Billy said. "Glad you could join us." We followed him into the Grand Ole Opry House. There weren't many people in the lobby and even fewer inside the theater. He led us to some seats about ten rows from the stage.

"Who's that on the stage?" I asked.

"That's Kitty Wells and her band. You fellas sit here, and if you need anything, come find me. I'll be working. Just relax and enjoy."

We thanked him and started watching Kitty Wells. I had no idea who she was, but Sid told me she was a legend in country music. She was old, but she was good. When she finished her number, I heard a vaguely familiar voice from behind us.

"Fellas, is this seat taken?" Sid and I both turned around, and if we hadn't been sitting down, we would have fallen. It was Dolly Parton. She could see the shock in both our faces. "What's wrong with y'all? Cat got your tongue?" she said, and laughed really hard. Then she sat down right beside me.

"Billy told me to come over and welcome you boys to Nashville. Is this your first time here?"

"Yes," I managed to say through my shit-eating grin.

"Well, where are you from?"

"I live in New York City."

"New York City?" Dolly exclaimed—just like they say it in those old Pace Picante Sauce commercials.

"Is your friend from New York too?"

"I'm from North Carolina," Sid said.

"I love North Carolina. And I love New York too. Now you two make yourselves at home. I've got to go up on stage and do some rehearsing."

"Oh my God, we just met Dolly Parton," I said to Sid.

"No one is going to believe it," he said. "We should've taken a picture."

"Damn it," I said, "I left my new camera in my suitcase."

"You better remember to bring it tomorrow night."

"I would've had it now if you hadn't rushed me out of the Days Inn so fast."

Over the next couple of hours, we sat back and watched a parade of Nashville's biggest stars practicing their songs for the next evening's show. Hank Williams Jr., Reba McIntyre, Randy Travis, Kathy Mattea, and the Judds. None of them came over to talk with us, but k.d. lang did stop across the aisle from us to tie her Converse All Star sneaker. If I'd had my camera, I definitely would have taken a picture of that.

If something like this happened to me today, I would have posted so many pictures on Instagram and Facebook that both platforms would have crashed. But it was 1988, and Al Gore hadn't invented the internet yet. Still, I did own the latest technology. The camera back in my suitcase was a Canon Sure Shot. It was so easy to use, even a caveman could do it. It used film, but was small enough to fit into your pocket. You can bet that I didn't forget to bring it to the CMAs the next night.

The rehearsal was surreal, but the actual CMA show was an out-of-body experience. When Sid and I arrived, we went to the will-call window to pick up our tickets. The person handed Sid an envelope. Inside there were no tickets, but instead two lanyards with our names on them. We ran into Billy in the lobby, and he apologized because he couldn't get us any seats in the audience, so we would have to hang out backstage during the show. "You'll have to stand on the side of the stage and watch from there." It was unbelievable. We had passes to walk around backstage at the biggest show of the year in country music.

All the stars were there. I'd been wrong: this was nothing like the rehearsal. Dolly walked by in an amazing sequined gown. Sequined jackets were everywhere. Everyone was dressed to the nines, including my dad. He wasn't wearing sequins, but it was the only time I'd ever seen him wearing a tie outside a funeral.

I spotted Dwight Yoakam standing against a wall by himself in a cowboy hat and the blue jacket and torn jeans he was wearing on the cover of his Hillbilly Deluxe album that had just been released. Dwight was my favorite singer in the world at the time, and I handed Sid my camera and asked him to take a picture of me and Dwight.

"How do I use this thing?"

"You just look through the view finder, frame up the picture, and press the button on top. That's it."

"OK, I got it." Sid said.

I walked over and nervously introduced myself to Dwight. I told him that I had just seen his show at Irving Plaza in New York City, and it was one of the best shows I'd ever seen. He thanked me and I asked him if he minded if my dad took a picture of us together. He said sure and put his arm around me. We smiled for the camera, and Sid took the picture. As he was taking the shot, Sid was looking through the camera at a strange angle. It looked like the lens was pointed straight at our crotches.

"You're shooting down on us, Sid," I said, "Can you see us through the view finder?"

"Yeah."

"Well, take another one just in case. It looks like you're focusing on our balls." He took another picture, but it still looked like he was shooting at a weird angle. I wanted this photo to be perfect because I was with my idol, Dwight. It wasn't like it is now with digital photography, where you could take fifty shots and pick your favorite. We were shooting on film, and we only had twenty-four pictures on the entire roll. So, you took your shot and prayed it came out all right.

I thanked Dwight and looked to my left and saw a very odd sight. Standing by the stage door was John Denver. In a tuxedo. I just never pictured the man who sang "Thank God I'm a Country Boy" dressed in a tux. But even more surprising was how much in real life he looked like Hermey the dentist from *Rudolph the Red-Nosed Reindeer*. He was all by himself. No one was talking with him. I felt a little sorry for him, actually. But just then, who walks by but the equally awkward Lyle Lovett. John Denver smiled at him and said, "Hey Lyle, I'm John Denver. I just want to tell you that I love your 'If I Had a Boat' song." Lyle smiled and shook his hand, and they spent some quality time together, both looking like Jim Henson creations.

"Did you see that?" I said, turning to Sid, who I thought was right beside me. He wasn't there. But then I caught a glimpse of him down the hallway, talking with the one and only Johnny Cash. Cash nodded, and the two of them walked out the emergency exit of the building.

What the hell? I thought.

While he was gone, I stood against the wall and watched country music royalty walk past. Randy Travis, Tanya Tucker, Ricky Van Shelton, Rodney Crowell. Everyone was dressed in their best rhinestone outfits. It was crazy.

Then I saw Loretta Lynn. She was wearing a purple-and-white sequined cowgirl getup with tassels on each arm. She was being inducted into the Country Music Hall of Fame that night, and I couldn't keep my eyes off her. She was a living legend. One of the best songwriters ever.

"Hey, there's Loretta," Sid said as he walked up beside me.

"Where have you been?"

"I went and smoked a cigarette with Johnny Cash."

"Are you shitting me?"

"Nope."

"Do you still have my camera? Will you take a picture of me and Loretta?"

I asked Loretta Lynn if she would mind taking a quick picture with me, and she said she'd be glad to. Sid pointed the camera at our crotches again and pressed the button. I thanked Loretta and went back to my spot on the side of the stage to watch Buck Owens and Dwight perform "Streets of Bakersfield."

A few minutes later—shit, I really don't know how much later it was, things were happening so quickly, and my celebrity stalker brain was on overload—anyway, Billy stopped and asked us how we were doing.

"Fantastic," I said. "This is the best night ever!"

"It's great," my dad said to Billy. "Ummm . . . when is Emmylou Harris performing?"

"Pretty soon. She's in her dressing room now."

"I have something for her. I brought her one of my pots."

He reached into his duffel bag and pulled out a box wrapped in Cedar Creek Pottery wrapping paper.

I smiled, thinking that my dad had a crush on Emmylou Harris.

"Well," Billy said as he looked at his schedule on a clipboard, "she's not on for twenty minutes, so let's go see her."

A minute later Billy was knocking on her dressing-room door. It was just like I had pictured they were like in Hollywood. There was a big star on the door, but it didn't say "Emmylou." I suppose on a night like this everyone doesn't get their own rooms.

Emmylou told Billy to come on in, and he told her that a big fan had a present for her. My dad was like a googly-eyed teenager.

"Hi, Emmylou, I'm Sid."

"Hi Sid," she said.

"I have loved your music for years and I just wanted to give you something to show my appreciation. I'm a potter and I made a vase for you." He reached into the bag and took out the package and handed it to Emmylou. She opened it quickly and held the Carolina blue crystalline glazed porcelain vase.

"Thank you so much, Sid," she said. "This is beautiful."

Speaking of beautiful, Emmylou was stunning. Her salt-and-pepper hair hung naturally down to her shoulders, unlike the rest of the stars there that night, whose hair was teased up high like giant tombstones on their heads. Sid was spellbound, grinning like our cat, his face flushed. I think this moment almost made him forget about meeting Johnny Cash. He stared at her about three seconds too long, then composed himself and said to me, "David, would you take a picture of us?"

Emmylou held the vase out in front of her in one hand and put her other arm around my dad. I pointed my camera straight at their crotches. Then I pulled it up and took a couple of shots of the sheer joy in my dad's eyes. It was so cool. I almost wanted to see those photos more than I wanted to see the shots of me and Dwight, and me and

Loretta, and of me and Hank Williams Jr. Did I mention Sid also took a picture of Hank Jr., and me? Well, I guess I just did.

The next day we got up, got in the car, and started driving around looking for a Fotomat. For those of you younger than forty, the Fotomat was a place where you could get your pictures developed in one hour. In the late 1980s, there was a Fotomat kiosk in the parking lot of every strip mall in America. *Twice as expensive, but a fraction of the time*, should have been their tagline. That morning we didn't care how much it cost, we just wanted to see those pictures. We found a Fotomat about a mile from our motel. We dropped the roll of film off and waited for the longest hour ever for them to be developed. We were dying to see them. I think both Sid and I were kinda in a state of surreal disbelief about what had happened the night before. It almost seemed like a strange dream that we had just gone through together. When we finally opened the package of newly printed photographs, it was quickly confirmed that it wasn't a dream. It was a nightmare.

At least from my perspective.

The very first picture on the stack of twenty-four was one of me and Dwight. The color was vivid. It was in perfect focus. We were both smiling. It was a great shot. Great if you didn't mind that half of our heads were cut off. I had no forehead. Dwight had no cowboy hat. I quickly looked at the other shots. Every one that I was in was cropped at my eyebrows. Not only that, but the shots were taken at an angle that made my legs look like they were two feet long. In a word, these photos were terrible. And I was pissed.

"What the hell?" I yelled at Sid, "I told you you were pointing the camera at my crotch!"

"I think they look pretty good," Sid said, shifting uncomfortably in his seat, trying to make the best of the situation.

"But you chopped my head off in every shot!"

Photo credit: Sid Oakley

"It's probably just the way Fotomat printed them. Let's take a look at the negatives. Sometimes there's more image on the negatives and they don't print it all."

The negatives were negative. Still cropped at my eyebrows.

On the other hand, the photos of Sid and Emmylou were amazing. In one, they both were smiling at the camera. In the other one, Sid is looking at Emmylou and she's admiring his vase.

I was happy that at least those came out so well, but I was still furious at Sid for ruining all my pictures. I really made him feel really bad about it. I gave him the silent treatment.

We left the Fotomat parking lot and went to Waffle House for breakfast. I didn't say a word the entire meal. After the waitress filled Sid's coffee cup for the third time, he looked at me and said with a grin, "David, you know something?"

I just looked at him.

"A photograph is nothing to lose your head over," and he laughed uproariously.

It was such a bad dad joke that I couldn't keep myself from giggling, and we laughed really hard together.

How could I stay mad at him? We had just had the most amazing father-son weekend ever. Even though the pictures weren't perfect, they were proof that we were there.

Looking back, I realize that the pictures *were* perfect.

Picture perfect.

But that still doesn't change the fact that Sid was a shitty photographer.

ACKNOWLEDGMENTS

Thanks to Maya Myers and Betsy Thorpe for their editing expertise, Laura Beebe for designing the cover, Mike Carroll for shooting the cover, Diana Wade for designing the interior, Heather Nikoncyk for being Heather Nikoncyk, Katy Spiecha for keeping me between the ditches, and my family for putting up with me and for giving me such fun material to write about.

ABOUT THE AUTHOR

DAVID OAKLEY has been telling brand stories at BooneOakley for years. He has won many prestigious honors, including the Kaopectate Award in the eighth grade for having diarrhea of the mouth. His first book, *Why Is Your Name Upside Down?*, is full of stories from his life in advertising. Despite this, he was recently inducted into the North Carolina Advertising Hall of Fame. He lives with his wife, Claire, and their dog, Walter, in Charlotte, where they raised Sydney and Lucas. He loves his family very much and hopes they still love him after reading this book.

CPSIA information can be obtained
at www.ICGtesting.com
Printed in the USA
LVHW021417301120
672997LV00005B/356